REFURBISHED
SOUL

"Once led by substances,
now a survivor with substance."

by

FRANK GARCIA

Printed in the United States of America
First Printing, 2020
ISBN 978-0-9600633-9-0

*If you sold your soul, could you
spiritually afford to repurchase it?*

"It's a wondrous thing, that a decision to act releases energy in the personality. For days on end, a person may drift along without much energy. Having no particular sense of direction and having no will to change. Then, something happens to alter the pattern. It may be something very simple and inconsequential in itself. But it stabs awake, it alarms, it disturbs. In a flash, one gets a vivid picture of oneself, and it passes. The result is a decision. A sharp, definitive decision. In the wake of the decision, yes, even as a part of the decision itself, energy is released. The act of decision sweeps all before it, and the life of the individual may be changed forever."

—HOWARD THURMAN

SCENES IN A LIFE

Gross, This Is A Hospital?

Loud honking, and me thinking to myself, holy shit that was close. In the near to now faint distance, a guy yelling, "Get out of the fucking way, asshole!"

I don't know how I got to this point, but I was walking, went to cross the street, paid no attention to the light or crosswalk, and I just walked in his lane. Unbeknownst to me, there was a truck coming really fast, and he had just missed hitting me by a few inches.

That's it, I said to myself, I need to get help and no not tomorrow, and not after my next drink, but I need to get help now! It was at this moment that I probably dropped two tiers of drunkenness from almost being hit by the truck. I continued to walk, but now it was in the direction of the closest hospital, it was just me, my favorite white with blue striped shorts, and my quicksilver beach sandals.

When I arrived at the hospital, I went up to the nearest employee, shared what had just happened to me, and stated that I wanted to quit drinking! The young lady nodded her head, said ok, and decided to walk me over to the ER counter. She then said, "Hang on one second," and then whispered with the nurse. While they talked, I went ahead and grabbed a seat and waited for further notice.

"Hello, Sir? Sir? Excuse me."

Me?

"Yes, come on up; have you been here before?"

No.

"What is your name?"

Frank Garcia.

"What is your social security number?"

xxx-xx-xxxx

"Ok, I was told why you are here, and you are also trying to quit drinking, right?"

Yes, Ma'am. (thinking why did she say also?)

"Ok, have a seat, and I will have someone see you soon."

Ok

(about thirty minutes go by)

"Frank?"

Yes Ma'am

"Frank, come with me."

We started walking down the hallway.

WTF? Did that chick just almost throw up on me? Wait, wait, wait, (as I began to distance myself from her) I am sorry, Ms., maybe I came at the wrong time, or perhaps this just isn't the place for me.

"Oh, I am sorry."

The nurse said as she continued to walk me over to the intake area.

"We get all types here, and we try to accommodate everyone, no matter how they are feeling, or what condition they're in."

Good enough, it's probably just me, besides my drunken ass shouldn't be here anyway, but like I always say, the situations we find ourselves in are more often than not the ones we created. Right?

"Yep, and well put. You said it was Frank, right?"

Yes, Ma'am.

"Oh, young man, you do not have to call me Ma'am but thank you. Let's get you situated right over here and get your blood pressure. After we are done here, I'll have you take a seat over in the lounge until further notice."

Ok, thank you.

The intake nurse proceeded to take my blood pressure and as you can well imagine, it was definitely high. I was still a little drunk, and I shouldn't have been wandering around the streets anyway. I went on to tell her that I came into the closest hospital because I almost got hit by a truck; I had thoughts of walking into a liquor store and stealing a bottle of liquor and a sandwich. Most of all, I thought since I didn't plan to, maybe this was the best time for me to quit drinking and rocking my illicit substances to sleep.

Earlier that day, after getting home from work, I just wasn't feeling it. Work sucked (because of me), and I didn't produce the way only Frank can, with self- pride and professionalism. Who was I fooling? Even as a functioning alcoholic-addict, I knew I would have more bad days than good? Nonetheless, I spared no time in reaching for the freezer handle, and BAM, hello Mr. Goose. I did this little shimmy dance I do when I get excited, went over to the couch, and finished approximately half of a 1.75l bottle of Grey Goose (yes, the Costco one), along with a few shots of Jägermeister.

I had to.

I needed to escape and fast. My thoughts were closing in with their ever so eloquent voices whispering, "Frank, you know you really fucked up as a husband, you can't even pull it together, and those beautiful daughters of yours, Puh you're a zero!"

I know, I know, I know, get the fuck off me!

I needed to fend off the emotional, combative darkness which often hunts me. Some days the voices win, and some days I do, at least I think I do.

Continuing on, I was five minutes into having a seat in the hospital lounge, and even a guy like me feels he is in the wrong place. For example, the older guy down the row and over to the right had no shirt on and rocked back and forth slowly with a numb facial expression. Second, the man in my left peripheral was sitting Indian style on top of the chair with a blanket over his head. Odd, right?

It gets odder.

Well, maybe not for the guy sitting Indian style.

A young woman sat next to him and within a few minutes, starts jacking him off, what? What's going on here? He didn't move while still sitting like that, and the light blanket on his head didn't move either. Where am I, I asked myself, attempting to try and sober up quickly?

I got up and walked over to the nurse's desk down the hall.

Um, excuse me, Ma'am, but there are things going on that do not seem right for a hospital. She made it very clear that where we all were, wasn't for normality in the first place. She went on to say that "Everyone here is waiting to be processed into the hospital's departmental ward, so just have a seat back over there, and we will get to you shortly."

Departmental ward? I'm sorry, what department?

"Psychiatric services, I was told you were having thoughts of killing yourself?"

Uhh, apparently this was one big miscommunication. When I told the intake nurse that I was almost hit by a truck nearly killing myself, she must have misunderstood, that I wanted to kill myself?

"Hmm, ok, well, just go back and have a seat, and we will get to you shortly."

Apparently, she was going to wait for me to be escorted by another nurse to the ward within the hospital, but in a separate building.

I went back to the lounge to find the guy that was getting jacked off was now having the same girl face down in his crotch area. WTF? The blanket had moved and was now covering her as well. Even by now, with only a buzz left, I was shell shocked. I quickly gazed to see if anyone else around was watching this, and no one really seemed to care. It appeared to be just another day in the crazy house waiting room.

I sat for another thirty minutes and went back to the nurse's counter. I said, look, miss, obviously, there has been a mistake somewhere, and I would like to leave now.

She said, "Hold on, Garcia."

You see, the reason I didn't just leave was that the doors were exit proof, and you had to be buzzed in and or out.

The nurse came back and said, "Okay, Mr. Garcia, I am going to have another nurse come and get you in a few minutes. They will sit with you and ask you a few questions. After that, they will determine our next steps, got it?"

Got it.

I waited about fifteen more minutes away from all the nasty business that was going on, and a friendly, soft-voiced Latin fella walked up to me and took me to a private room.

This nurse told me that he was going to ask me a few questions, and upon concluding, he would possibly allow me to check myself out of the hospital.

I said thank you, Sir.

"So, Frank, what brought you in tonight?"

I was out roaming the streets in a drunken state; I don't really know why maybe just trying to walk off some emotionally hurtful thoughts.

"How long have you been drinking, and not just today, but to this extent?"

Far too long, Sir, I know I have a huge problem. I don't run from what I've become, but not being who I would like to be, really fucks with me. So, I drink like crazy to escape, you know what I mean.

"I do, I see this quite often, and you are not alone. What would you say is the core issue for your downfall?"

I've broken Biblical laws, I knew better, and I know I must endure the repercussions.

"Ah, a religious person, ha?"

Right now, it feels like I used to be one.

"What do you think about most during your typical day, any thoughts of hurting yourself, possibly thoughts of suicide?"

My daughters, drinking, my ex-wife, drinking, my work, drinking, the girl I'm seeing, drinking, and so on, and so on. I'm drowning in liquor, and the emotions are pulling me under. Sorry man, I'm getting emotional here, and if I may, I would like to leave now. I need a tissue, please.

"I understand, how about you have a seat, so you can sober up, and I will check on you in about an hour. Is that ok, and do you have someone to pick you up?"

Sounds good, and yes, can you call December for me?

"December?"

Yes, she's my...

"Is that the girl you are seeing?"

Yes, and she doesn't indulge like me.

"Fair enough, talk to you soon, Mr. Garcia, everything will be ok."

Thank you, Sir.

After the hour went by, and I was allowed to check myself out, December met me at the front and as usual, greeted me with a hug and kiss. Just when I thought, well good for you, Frank, I started begging her to get me a beer on the way home. I don't even really like beer like that, but my body didn't want to come all the way down from its alcoholic perch.

December said, "No, no Frankie I'm not stopping, I just picked you up, and we can't do that. You said you wanted to quit and look at you!" I then turned her radio louder because one of my favorite beats was on.

I started dancing in her car and said, Please, Dee, just one beer, it's only a beer, I don't even like beer.

"Then you don't need it!"

Please, please.

"Grrrr, ok, Frankie, I'm buying you one beer, and that's it!"

Ok, thank you.

December bought me the beer and a big one at that. I couldn't even wait till we got home before I opened it and drank at least half. After we got back to my apartment, she did a quick sweep of the place to see if I had any more alcohol hidden. She found nothing and only because I found more intricate ways to protect my stash. She went to take a shower, and as soon as I heard the shower curtain swing shut, I guzzled some hard alcohol that I had stashed away. The whiskey that I drank was in my cereal box, I wasn't ashamed, I actually thought it was funny.

Today, I see that my actions were that of a lost person looking to reinvent what my dreams initially built. Both nothing and everything was funny; I tore down everything around me, I was an alcoholic moving to the puppet master's strings, I was just glad that the alcohol and drugs hadn't killed me yet.

And unfortunately, they were not done trying…

The Right Now of Me

No one claps when you speak of an addict or alcoholic. No one cheers when an addict's story doesn't end with a smile. No one puts up a toast when an alcoholic is simply MADE because they endured more and more for far too long. My words going forward are those spoken with braids of vulnerability and self-forgiveness woven within them. Both the addictive and alcoholic ways of life captivated me and owned chunks of my soul. Who was I, how was I, and what was to become of me?

I grew up in Silicon Valley, just fifty miles south of the Golden Gate Bridge. I'm a Navy veteran who married the most amazing woman who became the mother of my even-more-amazing two daughters. I rose through the world of Costco, then a medical lab, and started a promising job that I enjoyed in the automotive industry. I was prosperous, successful, and I was living the dream I had built.

AND THEN I THREW IT ALL AWAY.

I became a person renowned for drunken disappearing acts and pharm party excesses. I was hospitalized over a dozen times for everything from an overly slow heart rate (thanks to benzos) to a 51/50 police-escorted hold (thanks to booze) and all else in between. That was me, and not only did I walk through this darkness, sometimes I even gave guided tours.

It's not fun looking back at those perilous and emotionally painful days, yet I wouldn't trade the calluses on my soul for anything. My fight back from rock bottom is the very essence of what I have become today because I've turned my life around.

Do you ever feel like everything is spiraling out of control? Do you feel like you're at rock bottom—or at least approaching it really fast? How many great opportunities have been just an arm's length away, and then yanked from your grasp at the last second due to your poor decisions?

Have you ever endured a 28-day rehab (or longer) that cost you a butt-load of money, and gave your friends and family the false hope that it would somehow FIX you? Do you remember their disappointment or worse, do you remember *yours*?

How many times have you shouted (or at least tried to), "This is my last drink! I am sick of this, I don't wanna do this anymore!" How many times have you said, "Self, I'm done! After I come down from this high, I'm not doing this anymore!" How many times have you then ended up back in the hospital, strapping on another wrist band and oversized gown? Well, for me, it was way too many.

Are you tired of the constant binging, guilt, self-loathing, and self-medication to cover-up who and what you are now? How would you feel if you could get your life back under control, feel more positive, more enlightened, and more respected by not only your devoted family and friends but yourself? What if I shared with you how to make that happen? What you can change and what paths to avoid at all costs?

WOULD YOU LISTEN?

Because if you would, I'm here to share with you that you CAN do it. You CAN quit any time, but only if you *really* want to.

You can decide today to turn your ship around and begin to nourish your life along with your closest relationships. Listen, I know EXACTLY how you feel; I have felt your exact feelings along with thousands more just like them. But there is hope.

Imagine you're driving a car. You don't have any particular destination, but you are consumed with the desire to just keep driving, always pushing it, somewhere, anywhere. Lined up alongside the road, your friends and family—even "society" in general—are all waving their hands to get your attention, yelling for you to turn around. Roadside signs read "Bridge Out Ahead! Fatal Drop. Turn Around!" Do you keep driving until there is no more pavement under your car, and you plunge into the depths where there is no return? Or do you *make a choice* to slow down, hang a U-Turn, and alter your life's path away from certain destruction?

If you're reading this book now, you—or maybe someone you know—want to make that U-Turn. You can make that U-Turn, you really can, and I'm here to help. Because I was once driving that same personal car toward certain destruction, crashed, fell down, and broke all that made me. I then decided to pick up all the pieces, head back, and begin to heal.

I made the U-turn and scratched my way out of that bottomless, dark pit. It wasn't easy, but my fingernails have finally healed after years of climbing up from that hell I created. Why did I do it? Because of my amazing daughters and the people in my life who deserved more, they deserved a BETTER me, the best me I can be. More than that, *I* deserved the best me. Because I'm worth it.

I believe you're worth it too. You very much deserve the *best you*. If I can climb out of darkness more profound than any hole you can imagine, then I know you can, too... and I want with all my heart to help you start that climb.

Just be warned: there is no quick fix. There is no shortcut to turning yourself around, cleaning your life up, and heading back into the light. There's a perfect reason for that—you didn't fall to rock bottom overnight. That was a journey made through a series of self-possessed bad decisions combined with weak behavior. You can't undo that much work in a day. This will, indeed, take time.

It will take exertion, conscious effort, and overcoming a lot of painful self-realizations to get right with yourself, your loved ones, and the world again. But you *can* do it. I know you can!

As I write this, I am reemployed by one of the best corporations you can work for, and I represent one of the world's finest automobiles. It took me years to rise again, and I have also gratefully earned back a strong relationship with my ex-wife Christina, along with reclaiming a warm place in my daughters' lives, a place from which I had been rightfully banished.

Today I proudly walk chin up with my head held high; I'm a leader of men, a good father of two beautiful girls, and a great friend to a select few. I used to get cellphone calls that said, "I can no longer let you pick up the kids; you're drinking way too much, and I can't have you showing up like that." Now I get calls from personal friends saying, "Frank, can you come to the hospital and talk to my sister, we need your help?"

And my answer is always, "Yes!" I *want* to help, to help share and guide them.

I want to help guide you, too.

Join me as I share a cautionary tale resembling scenes like that of a Quinton Tarantino movie, about a fight to recover my soul that I handed over to the devil himself. A period of time I wish on no one, yet it made me the man I am today. Please remember one thing: this is my life. I *asked* for every bit of what happened whether I'll admit it or not. Fortunately, I realized that while we're still breathing, it is never too late to change. Take heed of my tale; learn from it. If you are looking for a change in your life, then *please* listen before it's…

SCENE I

Genesis

Born in El Centro, California, I was the first grandchild in my immediate family. As far back as I can remember, my family always thought of me as the one who would make it big one day. My mother, a single mom and the oldest of ten children, took that dream a step farther. I was to be the shining trophy that she could one day flaunt in front of the man who had left us, proof that she could make it successfully without him.

My grandparents were born in the Imperial Valley and would later settle in Calipatria, California, but my mom didn't want to stay there after I was born. She said she wanted more for us, and we needed to get out of the Imperial Valley. She made her way north with me; living in many different cities but none of them earning the title of "home." They were all just stopovers on our way up to San Jose. However, no matter where Mom and I landed, no matter how long we stayed, every summer she sent me down south to stay with my grandparents, aunts, and uncles.

Life was basically good, staying with all my young aunts and uncles. However, I always dreaded when my grandmother, who I called Nana, would take me with her to visit her friend Sarah. It was ten miles south from the town we lived in, and the one- hundred-degree day, heated up the vinyl seats in Nana's car. There was no A/C.

As we got closer to Sarah's house, my body seemed to slump down into Nana's front seat. I didn't like going to Sarah's, and her home was always dark and freezing inside. It didn't take long for me to think of her as some kind of witch. I'm sure other family members felt the same way, but family is family; so, I went on these visits with my Nana and always against my will.

As a youngster, my mother had always warned me never to let anyone touch my head; she believed that evil spirits could leap from person to person, and anyone with enough evil power could put a spell on me. So, I especially wanted Sarah to keep her hands away from me. After arriving at Sarah's, she would always try and give me a hug, so I gravitated closer to my grandmother's arms. I always believed Sarah, if she could, would cast a spell on me. A spell that would make me accept her evil ways so she could use me to get into our family spiritually. No way, that wasn't going to be my path.

Nana would do her thing, and not soon enough, we would be on our way ten miles back home in the one hundred plus degree heat again. I knew at a young age that I was blessed from above. Mom always said that the Lord has favor over me, and that feeling was confirmed weekly when I went to church at the Andersons on Sundays.

The Andersons, whom I regarded as very spiritual and soulful African American family, lived just down the street from my Uncle Daniel's house. Part of Mr. and Mrs. Anderson's house was converted into an Apostolic church, and many neighbors in the community attended services weekly. The head of the church, Bishop Anderson, was the first man that I ever saw help people discover the Holy Ghost and begin to speak in tongues. After many hours of prayer and seeking God, Bishop and others, allowed me to witness those in prayer begin to seek God in a way that profoundly warmed my soul. This was an incredible feeling and not one that many people my age had felt. In my eyes at that young age, the Andersons to me was a very Holy family; one that would continue to serve God each and every day. Every Sunday, the morning service began around nine-thirty, starting with two hours of worship, including a live band, and you guessed it, no air conditioning in one-hundred-degree weather. After the morning worship, the sermon would begin and continue until around one. During these sermons besides sweating buckets, I would often hear someone speak in God's tongue. For me, it was the highest sense of security to be in the Lord's house.

Once the morning service concluded, Mrs. Anderson's son, Big Walter bar-b-qued and we celebrated our church commune until about four-thirty or so. After having some delicious homemade soul food, you guessed it, it was time for the evening service at five-thirty, and it continued until eight-thirty or so. Yes, then Sunday services were done, and time for bed.

There was one Sunday morning, though, that will stick with me for the rest of my life. This would be my forewarning into the spiritual world if I had ever seen one. The morning worship had concluded and Mrs. Anderson began her sermon. All of a sudden behind us, there was this horrifying pounding on the door. I still get goosebumps to this day.

Boom, Boom, Boom, Boom, Boom

I felt my body tense up and the door flung open, Mrs. Anderson quickly yelled, "You get gone you devil, there is no place for you here!" This possessed woman who had been pounding on the door began to cuss at everyone in the church. Mrs. Anderson told all of us to please exit behind her out through the front of the church until further notice. Another young kid and I ran out so fast. We went to the outside of the church, quickly crouched down and stared through the yellow stained-glass window as this woman kept swearing. Mrs. Anderson started to walk down the aisle in prayer when suddenly this woman fell to the ground and proceeded to slither like a snake heading directly for Mrs. Anderson.

The young boy and I were both shocked and frightened at the same time. We couldn't tell what she was saying, but at that moment we could only imagine it wasn't nice. We had never witnessed anything like this nor such a demonic take over like this before. We stared and stared, and about two hours later, this woman began to cry and lay there limp as Mrs. Anderson kept the love of God surrounding her with a firm hug and quiet prayer.

My lesson then was; God is real, and so is the devil.

Mom and I continued to live here and there for a while, we also lived with some family in Turlock, and soon we had our own heated place there. It was a good-sized place, somewhere we could call home, although we were only allowed to use a portion of it. You see, our staircase led up to a locked door. The upstairs was off-limits to us, but I never knew why. My mom told me that "The landlord didn't want us up there, plus the rent was cheaper if we only used the downstairs." My mom never stopped wanting to get her own place, and she would always whisper, "Someday *mijo,* we will have our own home."

Our lives in Turlock set the stage for a period of being alone. My everyday life consisted of just Mom and me, and Mom did whatever it took for us to survive. Most of the time, she held three jobs and always made sure I ate something. When Mom was younger before she had me, she had attended cosmetology school in hopes of owning her own beauty salon one day. For now, before her big dream comes true, she would do hair whenever she could, as well as waitressing at a couple of restaurants to make ends meet.

We would eat whenever Mom brought home leftovers from the restaurants. I guess you could say it was like we had take-out every day, and who would mind that. The other good thing was that I didn't have to share with anyone. Funny thing is I still don't like to share today, except with my daughters Lauryn and Ysabella. It helped that both restaurants Mom worked at were near the house. When Mom got home, I made sure that she immediately sat down on our torn couch, help take her shoes off, and put her feet up as I went to serve her food. I always fed her first and more than I gave myself, but she never knew. Well, at least she never told me that she knew.

I didn't see my life as all that different from anyone else my age; there were plenty of third-graders also living with only their mothers. That perception of "normal" I had would soon change, the day my friend Joel asked, "How come your grandma stays up so late, we sometimes see her rocking back and forth upstairs in the window of your house?" I initially didn't pay much attention to his question and kind of just shrugged my shoulders, but as time went on, other kids asked me the same thing. That started my internal thoughts wandering. Hmm, I knew the house we stayed in had its quirks; but don't all homes? And of course, I had heard noises, but I had previously just shrugged them off as well.

However, one Friday night, as I was leaving for a sleepover with my friend Joel, it hit me, I finally saw what he and everyone had been talking about. As we were driving off, there she was in the window upstairs, an old lady rocking back and forth. I would even swear she was *slightly glowing*. I couldn't stop looking at her as we continued to drive off. At first, my mind was racing with questions. Did my mom know who she was? Did she know that the house was haunted? Did the landlord know it was haunted? Did anyone know? For a youngster like me, this was a bit too much to process, so I focused on what the Andersons had always preached, "Trust God Frankie, and he will pour his favor over you."

When I returned home later that weekend, I found Mom in the back yard and asked her if she knew about the lady upstairs? Her reply was simple: "Yes, I do, *mijo*, but the rent is cheap, and God protects us from all evil." She was right.

I knew we were guarded by the hands of God, so I had no reason to doubt her. Still, I was human and a child, so doubt soon came over me again. As time went on, the rocking got longer and louder.

One day a strange thing happened to Mom and me. First, I stepped on a wine bottle at the local park, which required several stitches across the entire bottom of my foot. While at the hospital getting stitches, I screamed so loudly that my mom couldn't hear correctly from that day forward. To this day, every time I see her hearing aid, I still assume it is my fault that she has to wear it.

Later that same week, Mom got a deep gash in her foot when a glass fell on the kitchen floor; we knew it couldn't have fallen by itself, but she too required stitches on the bottom of her foot—the same foot I had injured earlier! Was someone or something sending us a message? Especially now that I was onto the old lady in the rocking chair upstairs. Was it time for us to go, or was our faith being tested?

Our faith was being tested, yet, Mom felt it was time for us to leave.

Looking back over the years, I had wondered at length if this was when I first allowed doubt to creep in and lay dormant within my faith. It seems unfair for me now to blame the child I was for such things: so young, impressionable, susceptible to boogeymen, and monsters in the closet. I don't honestly know. But my over-analytical brain has always kept searching back through my dark journey for the when and, even more importantly, the **WHY.**

Why did what you're about to read happen? Why did it happen *to me?*

Ultimately, it doesn't matter, and I'll tell you why. Deep down, I finally realized that nothing happened *to* me. It all happened **because of** me. And if the rest of my tale hadn't happened to me—because of me—then who else would have been able to deliver my message to you? No one.

Life is But a Dream

One dollar and fifty cents, yes, that was all it cost. Every Friday at Campbell Christian School, right after mid-morning Mass, a traveling food vendor came by, offering what quickly became my favorite lunch: two hot dogs, chips, fruit, and choice of white or chocolate milk. I looked forward to this all throughout the week. Man, I *loved* that soft bread of the hot dog buns warmed so *perfectly*. Yes, the food vendor lunch was only $1.50, and the whole school would migrate to the quad area to enjoy the warmed hot dogs and ice-cold milk. I still think about those hot dogs to this day, even though I no longer eat meat. The thought of those hot dogs still resides within *the good ol days* file in my head.

I attended Campbell Christian School in the fifth grade, located in Campbell, Ca. Although a private school, I called the freshly-constructed building "home." Campbell Christian was the structure I needed in my life. My mom worked hard to get me into such a school, and I didn't mind that the school principal had a paddle, and was armed with a signed consent form to use the paddle when needed. I confess I was on the receiving end of that paddle more than a couple of times. Somehow, I never really minded it, though. I knew inside when I had done something wrong, and I knew the consequences. I got what I deserved... or, more honestly, I got what I earned.

The work was a bit hard and highly challenging at Campbell Christian, but I enjoyed the school and knew that all of my hard work would be rewarding in the end. I learned the books of the Bible, both Old and New Testament, and how to recite them within seconds. Each week we had timed contests, right after our spelling bee, to see who was the fastest at quoting each book of the Bible. I was quick and won a few times, but if I remember correctly, my best friend, Vince, had the most wins. Vince was fast, and I didn't mind a bit. After all, we were great friends.

Mass was held twice every Friday: once mid-morning and once in the afternoon. I always attended the mid-morning Mass, starting promptly at 11 am. I loved Mass; I loved the singing, the praising, and the closeness of my friends and fellow students. I also loved Mass because I knew the hot dog vendor would be waiting when it was over with more of those amazing hot dogs in the soft, warm buns.

But there was more to why I enjoyed those lunches. It wasn't just about amazing, tasty hot dogs—lunch meant even more to me because I paid for it with an allowance that I earned weekly.

The money didn't come from performing home chores; I earned it from working with Mom. She worked at a salon called The Heritage, inside the Town & Country outdoor mall, located just off of Winchester in San Jose. My duties were to answer the phone, wash towels, tear foil, refill products, tend to the ladies, and sweep around. It was money enjoyably and proudly earned. Later, when Mom moved to a different salon, I had the opportunity to have my own shoeshine stand. Yes, even as a youngster, I was making decent money and had a long list of happily polished shoe owners. I loved that job; I knew how to shine shoes perfectly, and all the nearby business owners knew and loved me.

To this day, I can still break down the process of a great shoe shine. First, wipe off all of the dust, rub on some shoe cleaner, apply a good coat of Lincoln wax, allow to sit for a few minutes, brush with a horsehair brush, and buff to a glossy shine!

During those days of my young childhood, I also found myself going to work with my mom's new husband, Jerry. He had his own roofing business with his brother Harvey, and Jerry would often wake me up early to go with them during the summer months. I can't say that I really liked it, although I learned my way around a roof and how to mop tar, as well as lay shingles, but it just wasn't my thing. I preferred going to work with my mom and or my aunty Chris at the salon she worked at.

Oddly, it seemed like whenever I didn't go to work with Jerry, my mom would find some small thing that I did or didn't do, and tell on me. "Where is he?" Jerry would sternly ask when he got home. "He's upstairs in his room," my mom answered. It always angered me that she ratted me out on stupid shit with no regard, and without a second thought, but I figured it was her way of getting brownie points within the relationship. This was probably another reason I called Campbell Christian, and the daycare there, "home." It was the one place mom couldn't say anything, and Jerry couldn't hit me.

When I was about twelve, Mom finally fulfilled her dream and got her own salon. Now unstoppable, and glowing with her beautiful blonde hair, and always fashionably dressed, she wasted no time and named it "Shear Arostigui." Mom used the silhouette of a pair of scissors and a black comb and displayed it over her last name (Arostigui) as the sign's logo.

It was a reconfigured older home that was dual zoned for commercial use which Mom had transformed into a salon, making it very home-like for her co-workers and longtime clients. The kitchen became the break room, the dining room became the wash/rinse area, the living room became the hairdryer spaces and the family room became the hair studio. It sat just across the street from her old salon in Town & Country, and right next to my favorite Bob's Big Boy restaurant. She had worked hard for many years to achieve her goal, and I loved doing all the tasks while working there.

My Aunty, Chris, also worked with us. She always spoiled me; the whole world knew I was her favorite nephew. I loved Friday and Saturday at the salon the most because they were the busiest days, and Mom's loyal customers regularly brought fresh baked goods to share with everyone in the shop. It was her dream come true, and the baked goods were just icing on the cake for me, pun intended.

I had a dream by then, too: I really wanted to become a pilot one day. Years ago, the San Jose Airport had an open field just off of Coleman Avenue; we used to park and watch all the planes take off and land. I just knew that one day I was going to be in the cockpit flying one of those big planes. Later, as a teen, I became enthusiastically involved with the Civil Air Patrol (CAP), an auxiliary of the US Air Force. I loved it. I believe it was during these years while in CAP that I began to learn self-discipline and a different kind of discipline outside of Mom. My squadron met every Tuesday night in full Air Force Uniforms to conduct advancement classes, drill, and to overall learn more about the importance of the Civil Air Patrol. Every summer in July the CAP would conduct a two-week boot camp down in Vandenburg Air Force Base. I really liked this phase of CAP, and I most appreciated the intense disciplinary setting that I was able to experience while on the base.

A few years later, when I turned 15, Mom told me she could afford to send me to private flying lessons. I was so excited and so grateful when she told me the good news. YES, I screamed inside! I attended a class every Saturday at the San Jose Airport. They offered a few different types of lessons, and my mom and I signed up with a friendly, patient instructor named Mike. I know it wasn't cheap for mom; the class was around $200-$400 a week, depending on if I was in class or flying in a fully fueled Cessna 172. My teacher, Mike, was so gentle with the way he taught me. I immediately liked and admired him. Lessons would alternate from classroom studies to the plane's parts and actual flying. It was tough for me at first, especially some of the math, but I quickly caught on. Mike seriously took his time with me, *sharing* information rather than just *saying* it (and for the way I learn, there's a *big* difference).

Almost a year later, after about 73 hours of logged flying time, I was suddenly pulled from the class because Mom could no longer afford the lessons. I was devastated. To be fair, it wasn't her fault; one of the harsh realities about marriage is that whatever one's spouse does, it also directly affects the other. Her husband, Jerry thought he was above Uncle Sam and decided to not pay his business taxes. As my mom put it, "Those sons of bitches are coming for everything. I have to pull you out of flying school, Frankie, I'm so sorry, *mijo*."

And so, I quit flying. I didn't make a fuss about it; it was what it was. My mom needed to help pay off the government more than I needed to fly the Cessna 172. Unfortunately, I met up with Mike one last time, and it wasn't for lessons, sadly, it was to say thank you and goodbye. That was the only time I ever saw Mike take off his glasses to wipe away tears. I had been his youngest student thus far, and I had logged more hours in a plane than I had behind the wheel of a car. I tried giving him all my school books and flight log back so he could pass them on to another youngster, but he said, "No, keep all of that, Frank, someday you will return. Good luck to you, young fella." I said bye, then hugged and thanked Mike.

I never went back, and today I realize that maybe I could have; I definitely should have tried. But I didn't listen to that internal voice of optimism. Instead, I listened to the passive voice of depression and self-doubt say, "Ah, it wasn't meant to be, Frank!"

Man, that is life's biggest lie, the lie that convinces each of us that quitting the pursuit of anything is okay. "It just wasn't meant to be?" Yeah, right, so weak!

On a positive note, I did hang on to all that learning material, and it finally came in handy. When I turned 16, I got my first real job at Costco. Later, one night, while at work, my friend Dominic and I were pushing shopping carts back into the store when he mentioned that he wanted to learn how to fly. I said, hah, really, you like planes, Dom?

He said, "Yes, and I was looking into the lessons offered here at San Jose." I knew the materials were expensive, so I said, *hey, I got you man*. I offered to give him everything I had. Fate? Yes, I think so! I gave him my books, measuring tools, calculator, pens & pencils, flight log, and the beautiful leather case that a lot of pilots use to carry these items.

Several years later, while I was awaiting a layover in Dallas, I actually bumped into Dominic at the airport. Wouldn't you know it; he is now a top-flight pilot for Delta Airlines. *Good on you Dom!*

My Time with Uncle Sam

On December 5, 1988, I awoke at 3:45 a.m. with a completely different attitude. Although still tired from the night before, I was ready. Today would be the day that I ship off to the United States Navy. It would no longer be 3:45 a.m.—now it was 0345 sailor.

I was supposed to meet my recruiter at the recruiting station by 0430, so we could head to MEPS (military entrance processing station) in Oakland. Mom tried not to cry, but she did, but at least they were tears of joy. My Aunt Chris (remember, I'm her favorite) was bawling, and to top it off, she was very pregnant. I gave them all huge hugs. My little four-year-old brother Eric would miss me as dearly as I would miss him, so I gave him an extended hug to hold us over until we saw each other again. Then, off I went.

I reported on time, and the other new recruits and I had our first muster (roll call). There were only a few of us there that morning, and after a short debrief of what the day had in store, we headed for Oakland. At the MEPS station, we were drug-tested one more time, had one more physical exam, and we were then sworn in. That was a long day.

I arrived in Chicago late in the evening at about 10 o'clock...
I mean 2200 hours. Being a Cali-boy, I hadn't really prepped for
the below-zero weather that awaited us. So needless to say, I didn't
feel tired since I was in a small state of shock due to below freezing
temperatures; with a wind chill of almost -30, and I had no jacket.

A shuttle picked us up and took us to NTC (Naval Training
Center) in Great Lakes, Michigan. I was assigned to Company 063.
Wouldn't you know it, the furthest barracks from the chow hall.
That meant it would be quite a hike in the freezing cold, a minimum
of three times daily, just to eat. Burr, I can still remember just how
the freezing cold felt across my face.

Except for the extreme cold, I was prepared for whatever the
military would throw at me. Calisthenics? I was ready. Making a
sharply measured bed? I was ready. Boots polished to a high gloss?
I was ready. The Civil Air Patrol had taught me how to be a sharp
soldier, except for the ironing and polishing parts, which were taught
to me by my uncles: who were hard-core *cholos* and highly respected
in our home town of Calipatria, Ca.

I actually liked boot camp; so needless to say, I did well, really
well. I did so well, in fact, that my folks were offered special treatment
and got to see me sooner than other soldiers got to see their families.
The Base Command also gave my parents preferential treatment
because they had flown further than any other parents within my
recruit company. I spent the day with my folks after our graduation
ceremony, but no sooner had they left, then I was headed for my
next stop, A-School in Lakehurst, New Jersey. We actually marched
and did calisthenics on the exact pavement that the Hindenburg fell
and burned down on. There was a lot of history here; I liked school,
and I enjoyed New Jersey. I was only there for about 90 days, then
graduated.

I completed school at the top of my class, and this enabled me the opportunity to choose my next duty station. I decided on the *USS Abraham Lincoln CVN-72*, the newest carrier in the fleet—although construction hadn't been fully completed when I arrived. We were not scheduled to be officially commissioned until late 1989, but there was still a lot of work for us to do onboard, dry-docked in Newport News, Virginia. Time flew by, and we were finally commissioned on November 11, 1989. Yes, Veterans Day, and what an extravaganza we had both on and off the ship.

A little more time passed, and we began our maiden voyage around the horn of South America visiting different countries. I saw many new sights, including my first donkey show (yes, it's precisely what you're thinking. I saw it with my own eyes in Rio de Janeiro, and it probably scarred me for life).

We made a few other stops in South America and eventually arrived at our new homeport of NAS Alameda in Alameda, California—just 45 miles from home. At this point, the Navy became like a "regular" job to me. I lived at home and only stayed on the ship when I had duty, about every third day or so. This was the life, I couldn't imagine anything better: I was serving my country, and I wasn't far from home. Unfortunately, this minor comfort zone wouldn't last long.

My Command needed to start training more with our Pacific Fleet. We had previously trained extensively on the east coast, but that maiden voyage was more of a shake-down cruise to make sure everything was working up to specs. So off we headed into the Pacific, the newest ship to join the fleet. Everyone allocated to our war group needed to get together and train. And train, we did.

I enjoyed going to sea. I served under Bos'n Henderson, a man with a solid attitude who made his men feel needed and a part of something bigger. He not only was a leader based upon his experience, but he had a very keen sense of every shipboard situation, the surroundings, and why we were doing what we did.

To him, it was simple: "Here you are, there is the damage; go minimize it enough to keep our ship afloat and your shipmates alive." I love you, sir; thank you for keeping us alive. I am proud to have sailed with you and Dino into the Persian Gulf War and make it back home.

The Persian Gulf War itself was quick, but the six-month deployments back and forth to maintain the peace we set were not. My shipmates used to say, "Man, I can't wait until this is over," or "What are we even doing out here?" I believe these same questions are still asked all throughout the military to this day, no matter what branch. My answer now would be the same as it was to my shipmates then: We asked to serve our country. We even requested months, sometimes years, in advance to join. Now here we are; we need to do our best, quit bitching, and serve our country.

I did my time happily. I served proudly for the freedom of Americans to do anything they wanted.

To Bos'n Henderson, thank you and "Aye, aye, sir!"

Times up Sailor

Upon my release from the Navy and a COD shot off of the bow of my ship (that means I boarded a C2 Greyhound, and I was launched from the carrier's bow). I wanted to take a couple of weeks off before starting my job and a new position with my former Costco team. My subtle yet comforting thoughts on my flight and drive home didn't last long, though.

I had my first apartment in San Jose, where I left my then-girlfriend Michelle the keys to stay there as she pleased. Unfortunately, due to my early arrival, I opened the door to find her and a guy watching my TV on my couch together. I immediately froze and put down all my luggage at the door before entering. I was cordial, I said hi to both, and as they started to create space between themselves, I brought my luggage in from just outside the door.

Now I know what most of you are thinking: Kick his ass man and tell that chick to get in the room and get naked or to just get out! Right? Well, I didn't do either, again I said hello, I am exhausted from traveling all day, and I would appreciate it if both of you left now. The funny part of that welcoming, or lack thereof, was that I didn't feel a thing. Nothing, it was as if I simply withdrew emotionally in a moment's notice. Perhaps I had seen and been through enough by now; maybe the universe was prepping me for more to come? Who knows? I just remember feeling nothing except being tired and wanting to be alone.

They both left, he left first, and she stayed back as if to try and explain. No explanation was needed, and I wasn't mean to her. I just wanted to take a shower and go to bed. Michelle left, and after my shower, I put all of her stuff in the dumpster outside. No hard feelings, I was just looking for a fresh start all the way around.

The next morning, I went over to my family's house to say hi, and plan a quick same day homecoming party. I hopped on the phone and invited everyone. By that afternoon, it had become a joyous day and one that will always reside within me. After a couple of weeks of doing nothing but hitting the gym, reigniting friendships, and getting back into a civilian mindset, I finally went into Costco and received my new work schedule. Wow, a civilian again, and no work schedule would ever be too much for me to handle. I was really thrilled when I later learned that my tenure with the company was actually accounted for since my absence was during a time of war.

As time went on, my schedule was gym, eat, work, eat, and work some more. I didn't really go out too much as a youngster in my twenties. I mean maybe twice a month or so I would venture out with my boys Ruben, Jimmy or my roommate Adrian (Ruben, Adrian, Jimmy, What up fellas?). What I did like doing, though, was having small house parties where I could invite those closest to me. That was always a good time. I dated a little here and there, and one time I even had a close friend of mine ask me if he could go out with one of my ex's that I had just parted with. UM, yeah, I guess? You're my boy, and of course, she is a good woman. I think you both would be great together. To this day, they are still happily married with a beautiful family, and I will always cherish them both.

I was young, disciplined, and ready for anything that Costco could throw at me. What made everything even more fun was I still had so many friends of mine around me. Years ago, I had gotten a couple of my friends from high school jobs at Costco. One is still there—what up Kenny, and the majority of everyone else moved on. As for the rest of my Costco team, well, we were just close! We did anything for each other, and besides, we were the Costco dream team, the ones who opened up California to the wholesale shopping world. Over time Corporate opened store after store, and they called on us to get them up and going. We showed the newbies what to do and what to look out for. Man, the good old days.

I mentioned close friends earlier and Ruby is one of those best friends. His real name is Ruben—my boy, my friend, my family and one very close to me. In sharing this with you, what I am saying is that at times, we were inseparable. We had similar cars, we liked to do the same things, and I respected him highly for taking on the role of Dad at 16 years-old. Yes, and to this day, Ruben is still with his high school sweetheart Lisa, and I love them both dearly.

Ruby believed in me, and he loved me enough to introduce me to his cousin Christina, who he got the job for at Costco. Christina liked working with us, and we all made our jobs fun and a good time together. Christina, then nineteen-years-old, was and still is an amazing person. She had these voluptuous lips, long dark hair, petite body, and was half Mexican/half Japanese. **Ka powie**! Christina and I became perfect friends. There was nothing we wouldn't have done for each other, and soon we were exclusive.

Christina and I were untouchable. It was clear within our crew that we were the best match made. Christina's aunt, Ruben's mom, Percilla, had known me from several years earlier because I guess my mother had dated one of her cousins at a young age. Who would have thought? With a lot of history tied into our acquaintance, most of Ruben and Christina's family knew we would not part. Christina and I were inseparable. About three to four years went by, and I wanted to secure Christina for myself. I was selfish that way, and I wanted her forever. I proposed, and *hello…* of course she said yes! I'm kidding, but I am very grateful for her saying yes and all she surrendered for us.

As the end of the 90s drew closer, it was time for me to leave Costco. I didn't go because I disliked it; I left because of the management at the time. I often felt unappreciated and without cause or direction. Before I left entirely, I attended school and earned my AA in EET, and I really wanted to become an engineer. This was my short dream at the time, and the course I wanted to run with Christina by my side. I commanded happiness and prosperity in our lives.

Upon my graduation, I was picked up by Coulter Electronics, a hematology company out of Miami, Florida. I appreciated and fully accepted the way my life was heading with Coulter, and at one time, I even wanted to retire with them. My job was hematology lasers and flow cytometry. I tended to most of the hospitals all throughout the bay area to ensure that their blood measuring/counting instruments stayed up, and functioning correctly.

Approximately one year into working with Coulter, the area manager called a meeting in Palo Alto for everyone in Northern California to attend. I showed up to what I thought was going to be a company get-together/update on the company's quarterly earnings and forecasts for Q4. It turned out to be a corporate downsizing and my last day. Coulter handed out dismissal forms to all of us. WHAT!! I was stunned, had never been let go, and to me, I was the best at what I did in the area. Yes, I may not have had the experience to feel that way, but if I didn't think it, who would, right? For that whole year, I gave all I could and showed Christina that I was going to be something more for her and that she would never have a worry. I wanted her to know that Frank Garcia would have her back forever.

I left Palo Alto in a funk of disappointment and embarrassment: How was I going to tell Christina? What the fuck was I going to do? My attitude was sour, and I whispered, I'm FG. I don't get let go! I took a long way home and I stopped at a bar on El Camino for a few drinks and to decide what I was going to say and/or do? Later, I shared what had happened that day and assured Christina that no matter what, I would take care of her. I still share that mentality to this day.

Christina and I were married in 1998, and things were amazing. Later that winter, Christina and I went on a family ski trip with her parents. On our way home, stopping to get gas, Christina said she didn't feel well. I looked back at her, she appeared a little off, and she said that she felt like throwing up and needed to go to the bathroom. Ray, her father and I proceeded to get gas and grabbed a few snacks before leaving.

A few days after we returned home from skiing, voila! Christina found out she was pregnant and not only pregnant, but she was months pregnant, which also meant that our wedding, honeymoon and everything else up to this day, was during her pregnancy. Myself, Christina and all of her family smiled, because the funniest thing was that as we were riding all of the rides at Disneyworld, on our honeymoon, Christina had a baby growing inside her. I didn't stay out of a job long; I refused, but now scared to re-enter the bio-medical field once more, I went to work with my cousin Mike in the automobile industry in Sunnyvale. Mike and I didn't stay together long, maybe a few months. My manager had asked if I wanted a promotion. After conversing with Mike about it, I opted to move on. I excelled quickly within the automotive industry and didn't have second thoughts of going back to the bio-medical field again.

I made good money; I knew what I was capable of, and I knew that I could, for sure, take care of my new family. Later that summer, Lauryn was born; it was July 21st, 1999. Lauryn was such a beautiful baby girl and still is, but she didn't come easy. Here is how that day began.

I was dead asleep facing away from Christina that morning when I awoke to a wet warmth all around my waist and thigh. My eyes popped open, and I thought, oh my God, I peed the bed? I quickly turned over to see what Christina was doing and to apologize for wetting the bed, but she was facing me with her eyes wide open and said, "UMM, Franklin, my water just broke! "

WHAT?? Let's go! Quick, Christina, you change, and I'll get your away bag and meet you in the car.

I scrambled around, changed my clothes, grabbed her hospital bag, awoke her parents, and off we went. We arrived at Good Samaritan and Christina was hauled upstairs after they called her doctor. The morning and afternoon went by and still no Lauryn. Funny thing is, Lauryn still takes her time to this day. Continuing on, as the evening donned upon us, Christina had been in labor for approximately twelve hours, and that's when the Dr. said she had to do an emergency C-section. Christina couldn't dilate naturally enough. I quickly scrubbed up, and I was able to be right there when the Dr. pulled Lauryn right out of Christina's tummy. I immediately went around the curtain to touch Lauryn before the nurses took her over to be measured and cleaned. Yep, yep that's my baby's soft little skin and as beautiful as can be.

A couple of days passed, and it was time for Christina and Lauryn to come home. I installed the brand-new car seat in my bad-ass ride, and off I went to the hospital. By this time, we already had our own place in Campbell, but it wasn't furnished yet. On the day that Christina gave birth, I actually went out and bought some furniture so that she and Lauryn would have brand new stuff when they got home.

We liked living in Campbell and enjoyed our neighborhood. We were centrally located near her family with plenty of things to do and see. This was our first place together, bought it with our own money, and we were now proud parents, yet because it was hot and we had no air conditioning, Christina's parents invited us over a lot. Besides, as grandparents, they wanted Lauryn around them often, and truth be told, I love my in-laws. Even to this day, both Ray and Carol mean so much to me—thank you for you, and I love you both.

Christina and I were loving life, we were both very compatible in a lot of ways, and we poured all of our love into our new baby Lauryn. I worked a lot, and Christina spent a lot of time with her parents. We hung out at my in-laws quite a bit, and they loved me just as much as I did them. While with them, there was never a dull moment and each room was filled with love, joy, and happiness. As it should.

Ray and Carol knew what I was about, and both had all the faith in me to carry out what was expected of me, and then some. They knew that the light from above shined upon me in the sense that God had chosen the right person to take care of their angel. I was greeted with Carol's kisses, and gentle hugs which held the power to warm my soul. Was I that guy? Could I go forward and fulfill the vision, they and I had of me?

The message was within me. And I spoke the Lord's language, yet, when he spoke to me, did I listen?

SCENE V

Lamentation of an Adulterer

For all that is secret will eventually be brought into the open, and everything that is concealed will be brought to light and made known to all.

THE BIBLE, LUKE 8:17

Christina and I lived in Campbell for a few years, and I excelled at work. However, our place didn't have A/C, and I wanted more room, so it was time to sell and relocate. I worked a lot, probably too much, but it is what it was. I made the money necessary for the life we wanted, and I was able to spoil my family. Christina and I agreed that we wanted to move, and I gave her the green light to shop. Christina found us a house pretty quickly, and in a great neighborhood where Lauryn would meet her lifelong best friend, Brooke.

After being married for a short period, everything in my life was going perfectly. I had an amazing wife, a beautiful baby girl, and a great job that was the first step toward a successful career. Top of the world, right? What could go wrong?

Have you heard the term "fall from grace"? It has its roots in the Bible, which I should have been reading more seriously and paying better attention to. The saying describes people who have everything and then lose it all, usually through selfish motivations and delusions. That was me. What happened next would become the blueprint for phony justifications and lame ass excuses that I would feed myself for years during my descent into hell.

So, what happened? I *still* ask myself this question. As I mentioned, I worked a lot trying to build a career that would allow me do whatever I wanted. At the time, Christina didn't mind; she knew I was doing whatever it took to look out for our family and keep us going. But while that was happening, I was becoming very full of myself. I began to convince myself that everything I had *just wasn't enough*. It was as if I felt someone or something had to pay for my brokenness as a little boy. I was mentally and spiritually lost in the wild, looking for who knows what. What I found next was the opening chapter to my own fall from grace.

I met a younger woman at work. Working those late hours, I allowed myself to get distracted from what was important. I felt I deserved… *more*. She knew I was married and—as odd as it sounds— she agreed that my family was my ultimate priority, they were first and understood she came after them. Armed with that caveat, I fed myself the necessary lies to believe that having an extramarital relationship would not take away from my family's time.

So, I did it. I did what was morally wrong, biblically wrong, and, most of all, it was the worst thing I could do to my wife and life-partner.

Remember, we agreed our affair wouldn't take away from my family time? That couldn't have been further from the truth. As my relationship continued, I would find excuses or just tell lies to see this woman a bit more. In a way, I believed my relationship with her became my first real addiction.

Why would I step out of bounds—way out of bounds—when I knew better? I wasn't raised like that! I had seen how my mother's boyfriends treated her; I, for sure, expected more from myself. I saw my mother's boyfriends do and say things that would have prompted me, had I been older, to punch them in the mouth. Those experiences should have been more educational for me, literally stamped in my memory. I should have been more attentive. Now, I was the person I wish I could punch myself.

I did all the mental gymnastics needed to persuade myself I was in control; I actually thought I could manage all of it: my family, my wife, my affair. I was convinced that no matter what I did, to who, with whom, or on whom, *I was untouchable.* I thought to myself, well, if I just do it once, it couldn't possibly hurt anyone except me. With that justification in my back pocket, I kept going. I don't even recall how I was able to swing from one mindset to the next and miss the chorus of angels in my soul, begging me, "No, don't do it! The Lord has shown you better, turn to him, and he will come to you!" I didn't listen.

So, I stole time. I stole emotions. Most of all, I stole from the "sanctity drawer" that Chris and I kept sacred. I was officially living a double life. When I was with Chris and the baby, I confidently felt that no one could touch our family unit. But when I was alone, I considered myself as a young, prosperous, egotistical, and untouchable man who deserved as much affection and attention as I could handle. (my real-life façade, a literal demon's oasis)

It was just the wrong kind of attention, and ultimately, I *couldn't* handle it at all.

I was stupid to think that no one would learn of my marital betrayal and my stained soul. I was so stupid to believe that the love of my life would somehow not figure it out.

Because she most certainly did.

One night while I was lying down in my marital bed, I felt this eerie thickness in the air. My body felt incredibly dense and weighted down. I couldn't move or close my eyes. Christina was lying next to me and began to quietly speak. I immediately felt that cold chill people describe when they know something terrible is about to go down.

On top of that, the virtual tightening of the noose around my neck was as if Christina's voice itself was both judge and jury. Her voice alone tightened the noose. I already knew that I was "guilty as charged" before she even finished asking me what was going on. I felt a paralyzing state of self-condemnation consume me; I couldn't move. I was completely immobile. All I could do was fold my hands over my stomach and brace myself, this was going to be painful.

Christina, her tone, both soft and accusing, asked me if I was seeing someone. My immediate response was the coward's way out: cast doubt on the charge by throwing it back at the accuser. Huh? What do you mean? What would make you think that? I asked.

To her credit, Christina maintained her strength and her composure. "I know you've been seeing another woman. I just want you to tell me, and I want you to tell me the truth. How could you, Franklin?"

That's when she started to cry. I had nowhere to run or hide, not emotionally, not mentally. And at that moment, I was overcome by a desire to comfort the mother of my child, and the woman I swore I would take good care of. This was the opportune time for me to come clean. But my shame overwhelmed my compassion, and I pissed the moment away like an ASS. I denied that anything was going on. I had been given a chance, to tell the truth, and I slapped it away like a buzzing fly.

I didn't sleep that night, and I doubt Christina did either. Morning finally arrived, and I dashed out of the house as if my soul were on fire. But there was no running from the guilt; there was no hiding place away from what I'd done. I searched my brain desperately for a solution while mentally kicking myself in the shins with steal soccer cleats. Inside I said, alright, Frank, you really F'd-up here. How are you going to repair the damage you've caused?

Ultimately, Christina believed more in me and us than I did, which brought her to the miraculous decision to *forgive me* and try to push past this. I knew I should have clutched at her unexpected mercy like a life preserver in a typhoon. I needed to stop cheating and do what I *should be doing* as a loving husband, father, and a child of God.

But I didn't listen.

I was never able to fully grasp the miracle Christina had offered— except her forgiveness, forgive myself, and try to move past it. I was grateful that she believed I would stop, and my clandestine affair would drop out of the spotlight. But I couldn't reconcile what I had done, and with how my wife had to feel about it. Inside I felt, Christina already sees me like a cheating man… so, ultimately, why stop now? That meant I had to continue juggling a lot of guilt and half-truths, which made me feel even more terrible. Ironically, the only way I could escape those feelings was to continue the affair, even at the cost of dwindling my time with our family. I recognize now that it was at this time that booze and I moved closer to each other, to the point that I welcomed the more than occasional buzz.

I took cold comfort in believing that since Christina didn't mention it again, she didn't know that I never stopped. Yeah, right, Christina was smart, and to me, a mighty woman.

Time went on, and I remember the night when Christina first told me she was pregnant with our second daughter, Ysabella. It was 2003, four years after Lauryn was born. Christina asked me to sit on the couch because she wanted to talk to me. I wasn't sure what to expect, but it definitely was *not* what she said. "I'm pregnant, and I'm keeping it. You can be involved if you want to—or not—but I'm keeping it."

Aside from being in a minor state of shock, I said to her, why wouldn't I want to be involved? Of course, I wanted to be involved, and why do you think she would present the news to me like that? Was it because I had once mentioned many years ago that I only wanted one child, simply so I could afford to give them the best of everything? That was just a worried Franks concern; I couldn't have been more thrilled that we were expecting again. Was she telling me that she somehow didn't care what I did? No, of course not. I knew she loved me; it was just her defense mechanism running that conversation... *because she very much cared what I did, and she knew I was still having the affair.*

(**Today**)-I profoundly apologize, Christina. You gave me chance after chance to make things right and continue on like the husband you thought I was, but I was too far gone in my own dark world. I cannot apologize enough for allowing the demons of infidelity, alcohol, and false psychological manifestations to run me.

Our second baby girl Ysabella came along on the 4th of November 2003. This time we planned for a C-section in advance. Lauryn even got to assist in picking out her little sister's name. I couldn't have been prouder to have two beautiful baby girls.

But despite that—or perhaps because of that—I couldn't have been less proud of myself and my damaged character. It weighed on my mind constantly. I started to convince myself every day that I wasn't the right person for Christina. I literally thought she would be better off without me; I wasn't available on weekends (she didn't mind), I hadn't shown her as much love as I should have, and I had betrayed the very core of our marriage and her trust through my infidelity. I fucked it all away. I refused to listen to the angel's voices within me that counseled, "Allow love inside you. Say your prayers. Continue to ask for forgiveness and stick by her side. Do-not-let-her-go."

But there was no shaking the ill knowledge; *Christina deserved better than me*. I told Christina that I had to go. And although I was no longer interested in a life with anyone else, I did my best sales job to convince her as to why she didn't need me. I told her that I would always do good by her and the girls, but it was better for her if I pulled myself away from our marriage. I walked each day as if a thousand pounds were on my shoulders, I profoundly didn't want to go, but the guilt bulldozed me over the curb.

And so, we parted ways... well, *I* parted ways from Chris and our family. She forced one final act of bravery out of me and made *me* tell Lauryn that I was leaving. I didn't want to have that conversation; I wanted to take the coward's way out so I wouldn't have to see the face on my little girl as I told her "Daddy's leaving." It *crushed me* to tell Lauryn, but I assured her that she would always be my priority and that I would stay close to her no matter what. (At the end of this story, that may turn out to be the only thing I did right.) I always lived only a few miles away so I could stay within reach of Lauryn and Ysabella.

So that was it. Done. I stood there empty inside. *Where do I go now? What do I do?* My inner voice—the loud one, the one who whispered delusions to me for years to come—tried to give me a pep talk. "You got this, Frank. You can take care of anything and everything from a distance. They're better off without you. Your sins have consumed you, and you can't go back now. You'll only disappoint yourself, and we can't have that." Come to think of it, that was a pretty crappy pep talk.

One spring evening, there was one final moment when Christina made a last effort to save "us." On that spring night, I stopped by to drop off Lauryn from being with her the whole day. Christina grabbed my arm and stopped me outside the front door and asked me to sit down on the porch swing. She told me that she had started to talk to someone, but it wasn't as serious or as important as *us*. Christina asked me if I would please come back. She asked me if we could work together on fixing everything. Who does that? Christina did, and the devil yanked me right off the porch.

I had already checked out on myself.

Please note; If you ever have the opportunity to save what you have, please do the *opposite* of what I did: get in there and do everything you can to keep your woman, your family, and your sanity. The alternative here may follow my path of jumping into life's blender. Looking back now, if I could only change one decision in my whole life, this would have been the one. My weakness was in not accepting her outstretched hand at that moment, which led to everything that followed.

Now, let me be clear about one thing: the cautionary tale ahead within these pages didn't happen TO me—it all happened *because of me*.

To Christina and my girls, in front of all who know me personally, or who are reading this now, I profoundly apologize to you. I am forever indebted to your grace.

Life gave me a clear message then, and I didn't listen! Sadly, for those who are close to me, my deafness wouldn't end there.

SCENE VI

Forfeited Soul

I t was in 2005. Christina and I separated and were headed for divorce. I will be the first to say that this was absolutely not her choice. I was the one who had promoted dissolution as if it would be a good thing for us. In reality, that was a cop-out and a terrible decision on my part. I had managed to still convince myself that because I worked so much and caused so much damage, this was the best choice for her; she deserved better. So, I took the easy "out."

I knew it was the absolute wrong thing to do. But I did it anyway.

I ultimately moved out and assured Christina that she would have no worries monetarily and that things would all be better without me. I was twisted inside, dark, foggy, guilty, but also relieved of the day-to-day personal responsibility, and I found that alluring. The first red flag?

Months would pass, and part of me remained pretty adamant about being on top of the world. My daughters were nearby, health, money, job, car—I had it all. I thought I was unstoppable… yet underneath it all, I felt more than ever that the Holy Spirit had just let go of my soul. Well, he did because I sold it, and I was on my own. When I stopped long enough to feel anything, I remember feeling so *lonely*. I couldn't stop thinking of my little girls. I remember one time I was on my way to see a chick (in my head, that's how I reduced female companionship... they were all "chicks"), and I couldn't stop crying. I stopped at one of my favorite liquor stores on Hamilton Avenue and bought a fifth of Crown Royal to get my act together. I drove around sipping away—after all, I was the man, right? *Dry those tears and ACT like one, Frank! Keeeep drinking.*

By the time I arrived at the chick's house, I was numb to the core from the Crown. Congratulations, I had escaped my real feelings, at least for now. I didn't waste any time; we did what we did, and afterward, I drank some more, and we did it some more. This was the lifestyle, right? I was the man, I was unstoppable. Give me a bottle, and away with the feelings.

I spent my whole summer riding clouds and trying to ignore or drink away my true feelings. It felt natural to me at first because I was killing it at work: I was on top of my game in my position. I had mastered the art of people, emotions, and persuasion. Later in life, I discovered that I could have become a General Manager in just a short time... but I fucked it all away.

POW! By that November, I found myself out of a job. I was shocked. I had been asked to resign because of a situation that arose when an employee had become sick on my watch. I failed to help her appropriately. Another employee stated that he smelled alcohol on me that night. That's exceptionally likely since I had become a daily drinker and had become used to the smell, yet I forgot that to others, it was an inappropriate smell at work. To top it all off, two female employees decided that this was their opportune time to collaborate and say that I was trying to pursue them. What? HELL, NO! This could not have been any further from the truth. Neither of them had been the focus of my attention; this was just their way to get back at me for shutting them down. One female with a manly stature that wasn't my type. Plus, come on, I knew she had strong feelings for my friend, and I told her that I wouldn't hook them up because he was married. The other female was out of bounds, and just not for me.

That job was everything to me, I, along with two great co-workers, had built a culture there that could withstand any storm. We together broke records and were undeniably on top of our game. Yet, I had to leave.

I bounced from job to job, which I managed well enough for a time. I, like the blood from a sinner's body, was flowing down the river of sin, drinking heavily, and started sampling narcotics along the way. Any time I allowed myself a quiet moment to think, I could only think about my daughters… and those thoughts sent me in a downward spiral every time.

Depression wasn't easy to run from, yet it was easy to mask—drink a little more, party a little longer, hook up with another chick… The state of mind became a simple matter of substance management.

The whispers were faint.

There was a message here, and I didn't listen!

My Stint in San Francisco

I
n July 2006, a piece of good fortune fell into my lap when I landed a great job in San Francisco. I regained the opportunity to be me, the motherfucker who can put it down from all angles. I was a true lion in a jungle where if you weren't one, then you better do your best to act like one. I could again work my magic as a top tier Sales Manager… at least that's what I thought on the surface.

I truly liked working at this place; the commute was an hour-long, but that just gave me time to plan out my day. My talents let me rise above all the background noise that said, "Who the fuck is this guy?" When it came to my job, I really did know what I was doing; I would raise the gross profits, put money in my teams' pockets, and make trustworthy friends whom I genuinely hold near and dear to this day.

I thought I knew what I was doing outside of work, too; I knew who to party with and how! I had a very select group of friends who I enjoyed a great time with, and who let me "be myself." I could drink as much as I wanted, pop a few pills if I felt like it, and go home with whomever I chose that night. That party attitude led to more than a few blurry mornings when I woke up next to a naked woman thinking four things: "Who's next to me?" "What time is it?" "Do I need to get to work?" and "When can I do this again?"

It was during these times that I started seeing a girl named December. She was suitably my type: funny, well maintained, stylish, and really enjoyed me for me. We carried on for quite a while, becoming accustomed to each other's ways. She was quirky yet persistent; she kept trying to change me but couldn't. As we grew closer, I even thought of becoming exclusive. But hell no, not me. I had to have whoever and whatever I wanted, whenever I wanted it. And deep down, truth be told, I didn't want to feel like I was replacing Christina. I just couldn't.

I remember one time when I went to Las Vegas with December and some friends. We were headed there to party and have a good time. After we landed, we grabbed a cab from the airport and checked into a nice hotel. As the night came on in Vegas, we could literally feel the excitement in the street. We grabbed a little food, went back upstairs to change, then went out to a club.

On our way there, December had reached out to a contact she had recently had a fling with—at least that's how I saw it. While at the club she and her guy (positioned as a "friend") were both dancing in the corner, and yes, this is the club that *I* brought her to; it was apparent to me that she had an alternate agenda. Through the fog of my growing buzz, I tried to get her attention, but she wasn't having it. *Oh really?* As far as I was concerned, that's not how the game worked—I was the only one who could do whatever I wanted. So, I continued to dance with whomever, and I was in search of the sexiest chick in there, just to get back at her.

I danced a bit with a few fine girls, then stormed out and hit up some guy on the street, and asked if he knew where I could score a hit of "H." He just smiled and said, "I got you, man. On these streets, you don't have to look so obvious, though." I thought to myself, did I look that obvious? Did I look like a stressed-out fiend, or did I just resemble someone looking to escape any emotion I thought to be real? I guess it really didn't matter; I just wanted to get high right now.

Anyway, this guy came across as a modern-day Willy Wonka of the drug scene. He sold me a couple of pieces of candy, and they were even in the tootsie roll wrappers. At first, I was like, um, what is this? To which he said, "Go ahead, dude, pick whatever you like?" There, in the bag appeared to be several different types of real candy. I said I'll take a few lollipops. After all, I wanted to erase the alcoholic breath I had. I paid the guy, unwrapped a lollipop, and stuck it in my mouth. My immediate reaction was somewhat neutral; I tasted the candy a bit more and then asked, what is this man?

He said, "They are real lollipops dipped in crushed oxy, you know, laced with painkiller prescriptions, and/or heroin on a stick." I was like, TA-DA!

Then he said, "Yea, it's a process, but an easy one. I unwrap the candy, dip them in water, and then rub them all around in different crushed drugs." I said, wow, ok, well, thanks. And we parted ways; now I had been introduced to a new type of drug! The CANDY did what it was supposed to do. I escaped the moment and December's abrupt, insulting betrayal. Fuck it! I carried on back to my hotel room and quickly passed out.

Morning came quickly, and I couldn't wait to get on that plane and head home. I didn't remember the airport or even taking off. I came to from a dead sleep and prepared to land in Oakland, and I still felt completely out of it.

After we landed, I got inside my car and headed south on 880 for 50 miles to San Jose. During the drive, I kept thinking, how could I have been played like that? I now understood clearly where

I stood with December, and I carried on smarter. Reaching out first would not be in my best interest. Besides, I learned early in the game that for every chick who gets away, there are more waiting just over the horizon. Eventually, she and I agreed to just be great friends and always watch out for each other. That was a better ending than I could have ever counted on, all things considered!

Sometime later, there was a big party approaching that became the talk of the dealership, a unique gathering that would involve a City Chapter of Friends and our dealership brand. I was so excited about the event because I loved to get dressed up and look sharp (I always referred to that as getting "G'd Up") and because I loved to drink. I knew the evening would prove to be a very memorable night, and I was right.

Just not in the way I would have chosen.

By the late afternoon, I had a room at the Ritz-Carlton in San Francisco. It wasn't too fancy, yet very lovely, and I had a good plan for the evening. Before I checked in, I stopped by the liquor store to stock up. I had a small after-party planned for a few choice friends and for one hand-picked woman to stay the night with me. I will admit this was one girl that I really wanted. I really had no intention of being too aggressive or pushing too hard to sleep with her. I simply just wanted her presence near me whenever I could; she was an absolute stunner, enjoyed me for me, and had a smooth vibe.

After checking into my room, I clicked on the radio, poured myself a chilled glass of Crown, and started to get G'd up. After an hour or so, I tightened up my tie, took one more shot of my lady in purple velvet, Ms. Crown Royal, and I was out. After entering the quick closing doors, I looked in the elevator mirror one more time before going down a few floors and exiting out into the lobby. When I got to the main entrance, I slid the porter a $50 spot and requested a taxi. I looked sharp, felt good, and I just knew that I would own this night.

I arrived at the dealership, said hi to some friends, and enjoyed myself for a couple of hours. The music was poppin, the ladies looked delicious, and my drinks seemed to just get better and better throughout the evening. I didn't even realize I was probably having more fun than was appropriate for where I was and what I represented. Yet, as captain of the alcoholic team, I would once again justify my drunkenness at a later time, just not now.

WHAT? Ha? Where the fuck am I? Later that night, I ended up in the shower; I was back at the Ritz in the room with December. This was **not** what was supposed to be happening! What the fuck? Despite my sudden realization, I got caught up in the moment and continued on with the shower festivities—I mean, what the hell, December was serving me up. We did our thing in the shower, then continued over to the bed. I began to remember faint sounds inside my head like some kind of banging and yelling. I had no idea what the hell was going on. I asked December, what happened? How did you even get in my room, and how did you and I end up in the shower?"

"Come on, really? Frankie, for reals, you have no idea what happened last night?"

No, I don't.

Why, what happened? Did I get into a fight with someone? Did I do something wrong? And how did you end up in here?

"Oh my God," December said, getting angry. "For real, you don't know?"

She got pissed off and asked if someone else was supposed to be with me in the room last night. I admitted it but didn't say whom. I was more concerned about the empty time in my head between enjoying the party and suddenly being back in my hotel room with December, in the shower. Then she gave me the shocking news.

"Frankie, you had gone to the bathroom at the dealership, and after about ten minutes, I ended up going in there to check up on you, then we were both in there way too long, and someone had to use it. Some guy knocked on the door and asked us nicely to finish what we were doing, but in your drunken state, you opened the door and yelled at him. You told him to quit fucking bugging us, and you slammed the door. When he started knocking again, you opened the door, then challenged him to hit you."

Oh shit.

You mean to say that we were both in the bathroom, and I got irate with a customer in the hallway? I actually did that and then challenged him to a fight while I was drunk?

Shit…shit.

I was still faced, numb for a moment, and didn't know whether to reach for my phone to call my boss, or start fabricating the next lie? I chose the latter and started thinking of how I was going to get out of this one. After all, this was not a good look for a manager of one of the most prestigious brands in automobiles, let alone Frank Garcia. As December continued to fill me in on what had transpired, I went cold inside. Eventually, some of it slowly started to come back to me. How was I going to face anyone at work? This wasn't the first time I had lashed out in a drunken rage, but it was the first time I did so in public. There is no way I would have wanted anyone at work to see that side of me! I dreaded finding out just how major of a fuck-up this was!

Monday came, and I heard subtle whispers about December and myself. I deflected what I could and had a sweet lie waiting at the tip of my tongue for what I couldn't deflect. Several days went by, and thank God I was a talented manager who continued to post good numbers because I believe that fact bought me a little time. But only a short time.

Eventually, I got the dreaded call, and the general manager summonsed me into his office. Of course, I explained that I didn't know what happened, but I thought someone had slipped something into my drink and that I wasn't myself after that. Little did anyone know that I had inside knowledge, and found out before our meeting that the GM had watched some surveillance video of December and me, but he never mentioned the tape or precisely what he knew. I wasn't stupid, though; others had told me what he really knew of the incident. I too knew people, and at this point, I could sense that he was still more about the money I produced for the dealership than for the stunt I pulled. I sincerely apologized and kept it moving!

You see, while building this life of drinking and abusing drugs, I learned how to make every day make sense lie by lie. I don't know if I was "good" at it, but I indeed became proficient. When people would gather at my desk sometimes, one of them might mention, "Wow, someone was drinking a lot last night!" Although I knew it was directed at me, I'd stay silent, type on my keyboard, and continue to chew on my gum.

It gets worse. About a month later, my daughter Ysabella was turning four years old. Christina was planning a big party at a park in San Jose and reached out to ask me if I could get there by five a.m. to reserve a spot for them to get set up. Of course, I said I would.

That was the wrong time to say yes.

The night before Ysabella's birthday in the park, my friend Carlos was having a big party of his own just south of San Francisco. You guessed it—I was there. I showed up with my two favorites: Grey Goose and Crown Royal. The party was a blast, with excellent food, pleasurable drinks, and a few chicks looking way too tempting. In the back of my mind, I knew four a.m. would come quickly for me to drive 50 miles to reserve that spot in the park. So, I planned to stop drinking by midnight to be ready by four a.m.

Great plan, right? It didn't happen.

My boy Barry (man, I love that guy), and I were sipping on cognac (instead) and Grey Goose, and I lost track of time. In fact, I lost track of everything and didn't come to until six-thirty a.m.

An immediate feeling of panic and failure set in. I was so disappointed in myself because I had failed my baby and the people close to me once again. I quickly got up, wait, but where were my keys? My boy Santos had mistakenly taken my keys home with him, so I had to call him, wait until he brought them back, which made me even later. I called Christina when I got on the road, and she was so **PISSED**. She couldn't even get the words together fast enough to let me have it, and finally hung up on me.

Now I was doubly inspired to complete this mission. Unfortunately, I still had to go to San Francisco first because December was with me, and I needed to drop her off at her car. Once I got her back to SF, I stepped on the gas and roared out of town... wait, the wrong fucking way! I ended up crossing the Golden Gate Bridge into Marin County. *What the fuck?* Not only was I beyond late and completely rattled, but I was also still buzzed from all the drinking and now heading the wrong way. Worse, a few cops had already looked at me funny. I was trying to exit quickly and get back on the road to San Jose. At one point, as I was turning around, a CHP got on my ass; that sobered me up real quick. I thought, oh shit, this is it for sure, I will get arrested, and I'll miss my baby's birthday. Sure enough, their lights came on, and my jaw fell to my lap as I started to pull over. I felt both sick and afraid.

Surprisingly, he whizzed right by me!

Wow, that was lucky. I continued driving the speed limit the whole way and had plenty to think about for the next hour. What am I going to tell Christina and my friends? Before I went to the park, I stopped at home and took a really long shower, put on some cologne, fly gear, and off I went to the park.

On my way, I realized that I didn't want my alcohol shakes to start acting up in front of people, so I stopped at the liquor store to grab a few minis (you know, those tiny airplane-sized bottles). But I didn't just get a few minis. I also grabbed a 5th of Jägermeister and quickly finished it in the car. My logic was that Jäger smelled like black licorice, so if anyone got too close, that's all they would smell.

I arrived at the park, and a very pissed-off Christina marched toward my car. I rolled down the window, but before I could say a word, she let me have it. "Leave, just leave. Get the hell out of here, Franklin!" she said. "I don't want you here or near the baby when you're like this. You're drunk, I can see it in your eyes!"

I lied and said I had simply overslept, and I begged Christina to let me stay.

To this day I don't know why she changed her mind, but she finally agreed then asked me to go buy her some ice. Feeling like I had a second chance, I went to the closest market. As I pulled up into a parking spot, one of my favorite songs came on, so I didn't get out of the car right away. Boom, the 5th of liquor hit me.

Shit!

That was the last thing I remembered until I woke up to a hard banging on my car windshield. "Wake up!" my mother-in-law Carol yelled. "What are you doing?" I had no idea what was going on, and I was scared shitless. With the car still running, I was passed out, so embarrassed, disappointed in myself, and now I was even in more trouble with Christina. Carol had gone to the same store to get the ice I was supposed to be getting, and thinking I was not returning, she found me. Carol left me there and continued on.

I shut the car off and tried to shake off this drunkenness before getting back to the party. After a few minutes, I went back and parked down the street from the party and decided to just relax and shake off the rest of the buzz a little more. After about an hour, Christina let me back in. I was so excited. For a short time, I remember feeling like I was a part of something again instead of a fuck up. The party went on, and I could mingle with everyone, but more importantly, my little girls, but Christina watched me like a hawk. I knew these people were aware of my alcoholism, and that just magnified my shame and embarrassment.

Fortunately, Christina's kindness that day—as guarded and reluctant as it might have been—would help her play a significant role in sewing the proper seeds that have grown between my daughters and me today. Once again, she thought the bigger picture and outside of her own feelings.

Back at work the next day, I learned that although my numbers were above par at the dealership, they needed to close one of the stores. I had made it easy for them to downsize to one sales manager. Downsized? *Terminated! Was how I saw it?* I was told it was only because of seniority, but I knew inside I was seen as a liability to the company. I was crushed. I didn't know what to think. At first, I wanted to fight for myself and demand that I be kept because of my production, yet I could hear the little voice whispering to me" It's payback once again for my wrongdoings. You play hard, Frank, and you have to know life will play hard too."

Although I was a drug-using alcoholic, I understood life's rules: you get back in direct proportion to what you put in. At that point, I was putting in nothing but bad behavior. My withdrawals had superseded my deposits, and I realized my addictions had come to collect one more job from me. So, again feeling lonely and out of a job, I wasted no time in finding the nearest bar to drown out my feelings.

The message was clear, and still, I didn't listen!

The Interim (Part One)

I couldn't find work for three months. I bounced around looking, barely surviving; supporting Christina and the girls with the remainder of my 401K and the little money I had saved. Despite everything around me, I profoundly knew that—no matter what—Christina and my girls would monetarily always be my first priority. Even through all of this, I was grateful that Christina still allowed me to see the girls, but no sooner than I dropped them off, it was always time for pills and more liquor. I drank every day, all day. I knew all of the shortcuts to stay off of the main streets, I didn't want to get pulled over, and I always used my alternate routes to the local liquor stores.

I was a mess.

I was in a horrible place that I nicknamed "The Interim." Here It was dark, I felt lost, and I was torn mentally, physically, and most of all, emotionally.

Within the Interim, I stayed emotionally crushed every day. Suicidal thoughts ran rampant across the highway within my head. It was a fight, one side said: "It's better for everyone involved, you're worth more in insurance money, and time will heal everyone."

To which the other side, rang out "Haven't you caused enough damage, does Christina really need that on her plate as well, and is that how you really want your girls to remember you?" At the time, I didn't care for logic, the pain was excruciating and often very tough to manage. I did what I could, and along with that managed my alcoholism by drinking in the morning before doing anything. Yes, that even meant before going to see my girls. Lord forgive me, I got good at drinking just enough not to have the alcoholic tremors in front of them or Christina. But whenever my girls came near me, I could feel the tears of self-disappointment erupting inside me. I was so hurt, so disappointed, and I wanted everything back; my life, my sanity, my girls, and yes, as much as I pushed her away, Christina too. I have mad love for her, and I give her so much credit because even though we had gone our separate ways, she knew, she ultimately knew that I was dying inside, and she knew I needed my girls close to me. Thank you, Chris... with your mature kindness, you helped keep me alive.

Here's just one example of her kindness; Christina invited me to my daughter Lauryn's soccer game. As I watched my daughter play, Christina motioned for me to come over to her. I questioned it for a moment, like are you talking to me? She again motioned to come over to her. As I got closer to her, I said, hey, what's up?

"Franklin, what the hell happened to you?" She asked, pointing at my waistline, near the front of my front right belt loop.

"Your jeans are all bloodied."

I looked down. Oh shit, I don't know.

She gave me a questioning look. I paused, wondering if this was a good time to lie, but that was only a knee jerk reaction, in this case, I had no reason to lie, or maybe I did. I had lied too many times already so, this would be par for the course, but by now, I found it really difficult to lie to Christina anymore. Maybe my respect for what she was to me, simply took over. So, I told her the truth; I was drinking earlier, and when I left to come over here to the soccer game, I walked out and realized that I forgot my house keys. So, I climbed my neighbor's fence below me to gain access to my balcony, which was about five feet higher than his patio fence. As I readied to throw my legs up; I grabbed my patio fence above, jumped with everything I had, lost my grip and fell back down sideways on top of the neighbor's fence, bending my body in half and badly scraping my hips, thighs and pelvic area. Thank God I made it up to the balcony the second time without further punctures or injuries. I didn't realize the extent of my injury because I was already buzzed and didn't really feel the pain; Christina knew, yet still allowed me to stay for Lauryn's game. Thanks, Chris.

It is often said that the more you drink, the more your body adapts to handle more. For me, liquor became a daily regimen of at least a fifth of Crown or a liter of Grey Goose a day just to feel like myself. It was easy, and I quickly learned how to use both drugs and alcohol to medicate myself in different ways:

» I learned to use painkillers to knock out the back pain.

» I learned to use painkillers to escape my depression about not being around my girls.

» I learned to use painkillers to pass the time, slowly killing myself.

» I learned to use alcohol to have better/longer sex... or so I thought. (sinful shallow thinking)

» I learned to use alcohol as an escape from my daily sadness, thus prolonging any suicidal thoughts I carried with me.

» I learned to use alcohol to make sense of everything wrong with me.

»   I learned to exist without love, even with these known sins of mine, so I could better cope with my wrongdoings.

»   I formed an algorithm that if I didn't have feelings, no one could hurt them, and if I kept a tin man's heart, then I couldn't offer to love because tin man didn't have one.

I was sad day in and day out. I often said to myself that I was worth more to my girl's dead than alive. Nonetheless, I learned to cope with the existence I had brought upon myself. I felt I couldn't think straight until I drank to make sense of everything. It was at this point that my thoughts grew separate from reality. I was often in a state of paranoia. I always looked over my shoulder, through my rearview mirror, and outside the front windows of my apartment. I remember finally realizing how sick and tired I was of the constant paranoid delusional state that I always felt.

"**That's it**!" I screamed in my living room. "I'm not fucking doing this anymore! I am stronger than any substance that can do me harm."

At that moment, I quit cold turkey. I knew inside that my Christian upbringing could conquer the devil's demons within me. But I didn't know of anyone who drank or did drugs like me, so I had no one to ask for advice. I went into a short phase of dry heaving and throwing up yellow material; I later learned that I was actually throwing up my stomach lining. I felt cold and clammy, but at the same time, I was sweating profusely. This was my welcome to the initial stages of withdrawal. My body was screaming for more of something, anything!

"Please, Frank. Please, Frank! Give me *anything*. Just one more time, and you can quit later," the demons pleaded within me. The demons within were top negotiators, they would use a mass blitz on my mind to persuade me back, this was getting real, real fast.

Detox hit me hard. I felt something was off inside, and since I had no experience with this, I was super scared. I was told by a doctor that you could kill yourself if you didn't quit substance abuse with medical assistance, and that thought hounded me. I began to feel really dizzy; I didn't know what was happening, and I then started to shake really bad. I panicked and ran to the liquor store to grab a mini Jäger. I downed it before I even got outside. I felt terrible the whole way home, terrible... but within minutes, I started to feel better. I went to bed and actually remember telling myself to look forward to a better day when I woke up. Go to sleep Frank, go to sleep.

Morning came, and so did more of the same: more throwing up, and now the shakes began to set in, only now, just a little harder.

I told myself that today was another day, and I was strong enough *not* to drink or pop a pill. By now, I had nothing left in my house, not even in my secret stashes. This included the stack of mini-bottles that I kept inside my vacuum's bag holding compartment. Yes, I also used my vacuum to hide bottles from December. This day, I took a more extended shower than usual and got ready. I wanted to look good, so I put on one of my favorite suits. A nice power tie, and off to work, I went. I remember greeting my first appointment in the morning. After a brief greeting, I went to get a key to a car for my presentation, but suddenly I felt like shit. I needed to sit down... but I had a customer waiting on me outside! So, I shrugged off my body's warning, I grabbed the key and walked out of the building toward my customer, but something didn't feel right—*the fucks happening right now?*

My vision fogged over, oh no.

BOOM! POW! I've just had a withdrawal seizure, yes, a seizure, and I regained consciousness while lying on the ground in front of the buildings receiving door. I could vaguely see people trying to get me to look them in the eyes, but I couldn't focus. My co-workers were trying to figure out what the hell just happened. People kept touching me to see if I was good, but with each touch, I was in more pain. My surroundings weren't even in focus until I was lifted into the ambulance.

"Frank," I heard. "Frank, can you hear me? Squeeze my hand. Frank, you had a seizure, and you are now on your way to the hospital. Can-you-hear-me?"

I couldn't really talk. I didn't know what was going on.

A seizure?

What's that?

My mouth was full of blood, and my tongue had swollen to twice its size because I'd bitten down on it really hard. I was both seriously scared and colossally embarrassed at the same time. Funny thing is, I even thought about the customer that I didn't get to sell a car to. By now, I felt like I had been hit by a truck; my body was in pain everywhere; I was one gigantic ache. The doctor would later tell me that while I was having the seizure, my body constricted just about every muscle I have. No wonder I was so sore.

I arrived at Good Samaritan Hospital and was brought to the closest room available. As the paramedics transferred me from their gurney to the hospital's gurney, I could feel my body flex and cause me to squint from the soreness. A nurse tended to me and said that the doctor would be in shortly. Several tests were performed, and nurse after nurse kept coming in to check on me. After about an hour, a doctor whom I'll never forget walked in and introduced himself. "Hi, my name is Dr. Jerry Callaway." Dr. Callaway wore an old dingy Navy baseball cap, and didn't say anything after the introduction, he then quickly pushed his hand and the tips of his fingers into my lower-right abdomen.

"Frank, do you drink at all?" he asked.

No sir, I quickly lied. Well, just a drink here or there, nothing big though doctor.

He didn't buy that for a second. "Just a little here and there, huh?" (I would later learn that he didn't just feel if I had a sore abdomen, he was checking for a swollen liver, a symptom of alcoholism.)

Dr. Callaway immediately knew what was going on—not just from the test results and my inflamed and swollen liver, but all the other signs of a hardcore alcoholic, which he knew all too well because he was a recovering alcoholic of several years himself. Yes, I picked the wrong guy to lie to. What timing. Who would have thought? Perhaps it was more than just "good timing," perhaps even fate, as Dr. Callaway had actually been off that day but was asked to cover for a doctor who was ill. Dr. Callaway knew all about alcoholism from both sides. To this day, I will never forget his soft voice and comforting hands.

Later that same day, I was released, and for the next few days, I was still sore all over, but I wasn't going to let either stop me from going to work. I re-committed myself again to stop drinking. I consulted my family physician, Dr. Lee, explaining my seizure and describing how my lower back conditions were getting worse. I felt I needed something stronger for pain. Dr. Lee was kind enough to prescribe me a stronger medication, which kick-started me into learning more about synthetic heroin and its uses throughout pain management.

Money was tight, but I had to do anything I could to ensure that my girls were taken care of. So, since I could no longer afford the expensive prescriptions, I found myself searching for *alternate* forms of medication. I did what I could to stay liquor sober, but I was in massive denial. I thought if I could stay with pills, not only would it help the pain, but it would also help in staying liquor sober. It wasn't long before I was hitting up Dr. Lee more often than I was supposed to. I would tell him things like; the latest prescription didn't really work, I lost the last order, or I left my prescription at the gym. Once, I even told him I left my medicine in a car that I traded in. They were all lies, but I received a refill after refill. Nevertheless, at the same time, I was re-training my body for the returning demons. After all, they were the yard duty during my recess.

It wasn't long before Dr. Lee grew suspicious, and thus, it was time to find a new doctor and get acquainted with more people in the street pharmacy trade.

About a month went by before I realized that I could piggyback a pill with a drink and amplify the results—with sometimes bizarre results. By now, I could master self-medication and take it to the next level. I began drinking again, but this time I was not going to act like a real alcoholic. So, I just sipped here and there with the mindset that it's only a little, and besides, I'm in control. Yep, one small drink here and there led to more in the morning, noon, and night, with pills all throughout, and nothing was going to stop this train. Fuck! This hurts to admit, but inside of me was a fully functioning substance abuser. Yes, I was an abuser day in and day out.

I had arrived again.

A few months would go by, and one day after regaining consciousness, I didn't know what I had done the night before. That scared me into feeling I needed to stop this again. I was literally sick and tired of being sick and tired. I walked a few miles to Dr. Callaway's office, but there were no appointments available. I told the lady at the front desk (I thought of her as "The Gatekeeper" at the time) that I would be sitting right over there in that corner until he was available. I passed out in the waiting room from drinking on the way there. I laid there in the chair until I was awakened by Dr. Callaway.

"Welcome home," were the first words out of his mouth before he gave me an extended hug. Now I felt safe, not shunned like a trespasser. Dr. Callaway escorted me to his office, asked me to sit upon the table, and took my vitals. I remember his office was a mess; I thought he must either be really unorganized or very busy. He admitted to a little of both; nonetheless, he counseled me for about a half-hour, prescribed me Gabapentin, and sent me on my way. Before I left, I asked if I could get addicted to this new prescription. "Oh no, you can't get addicted to this," he said. "It is an anticonvulsant that will help prevent you from having another seizure while your body detoxes off of the alcohol." Ok, doctor, thank you, Sir, and take care.

Gabapentin gave me crazy dreams. Not bad ones, but really vivid and continuous; I could wake up, go the restroom, back to bed, and then continue with the dream right where I left off. It wouldn't be long before I started going to sleep earlier, and I looked forward to the dreams I would have. I would later learn that the Neurontin within the drug acts like a fiber-optic cable that tries to reconnect the neuro wiring within the frontal lobe "upstairs," which my prolific drinking had severed. I drank so much that I actually disrupted my neuro wiring in my frontal lobe. In time, I would later see that repaired.

Once again, the message was clear, and I didn't listen!

Steel Bracelets

A few more months went by, and although I was still sober, I didn't have control of my thoughts, let alone where I was headed in life. The devil, like some kind of composer of the symphony in my head, continued to play the oh-so aliquant music, which was both soothing and alluring to me. One day, as the sun began to shine through my blinds, I thought it would be a great day to go over the hill to Santa Cruz. I knew I couldn't see the girls and that bothered me, so I began to sip. I sipped on a couple of drinks while watching cartoons and making myself a little breakfast. After I ate, I stopped drinking and sat around for a few hours. When I thought I was good, I got dressed, grabbed my keys and off I went. As I was driving south on highway 17, I thought since I didn't really know the streets of Santa Cruz too well, maybe I should pull over and grab a little something to drink and take it with me. You know, take the edge off.

This was the wrong decision, or was it?

The next thing I remembered was a little bit of yelling and then a police officer barking, "Sir, I'm going to have to place you under arrest!" "Sir, Sir!"

Huh? For what Officer?

I know a lot of you may be thinking, "Oh shit, Frank's getting a DUI?" Come on now, what kind of alcoholic do you think I am? I stopped drinking after I had breakfast, remember. Well, maybe I didn't wait long enough before I left.

"Sir, we received a call from the store owner who said you were acting a little combative here. I can tell by the odor on your breath, that you have had a bit too much to drink," the police officer said.

Hmm, well OK then, can I just leave the store? I asked.

"No, sir. How did you get here?" the police officer asked.

Even while drunk and pissed off, my lying ability went on full alert. Officer, I was with some friends down the street at Vasona Park. We needed some more ice for our barbeque, so I walked over here.

"Well, as I said, sir, you are under arrest." He stated again.

He read me my rights and stated I was being taken downtown San Jose for public intoxication. I sighed heavily, and as I was being escorted out, I glanced briefly over at my parked car and hoped they wouldn't figure out it was mine. I cooperated fully, like I had a choice in cuffs, right?

On the trip downtown, the officer told me what to expect next. "I'm just going to take you down to intake where you'll be booked into jail. Once you have sobered up, they'll let you go. You will get a court date notification in the mail, so don't ignore it!"

Once at the jail, I was fingerprinted and had my "yearbook photo" taken—better known as a mug shot. I was told to "sit down and relax until my name was called. I fell asleep on the holding chairs yet, remained wide awake in the jail cell by myself. All I could think was, what the fuck am I doing here? Christina is going to have a field day with me! Here we go, man, here's another thing she's going to have on me!

By then, it was late afternoon, and I had only been there a few hours. I asked if I could go, but was told that I needed to stay here for a minimum of 6-8 hours! This was the protocol so that they knew I was sober enough to leave. Finally, just before midnight rolled around, the officer approached me and sparked up a light conversation. I guess he determined that I was sober enough to be let go. He said, "It appears you are good now, give us a few more minutes, and we will process you out." A little time passed, my name was called, and the cell door opened. I trotted on over to be processed out, and about 30 minutes later, I was let go through the Taylor Street exit.

It was a pleasant June evening, and the temperature was just right. I wondered how I was going to get my car. I double-checked my pockets to make sure that I had everything I started with. I had some money on me, and thought about calling a cab, but first… I needed a drink. I mean, *I really did*. After being arrested, who wouldn't need a little something to relax their nerves? So, that was it: I was on a mission, again.

I began to walk west of the police department, and I soon realized that I had walked all the way down Taylor Street looking for a store. I knew time was running out because no one would serve alcohol after 2 a.m. As I approached The Alameda, I quickly needed to regain my sense of direction and then headed north toward Santa Clara University. I was sure I could make it by 2 a.m. to pick up some Crown Royal at Safeway by the campus. I have to have it. I have to have it. Oooh, I can't wait until I can get my lips around that bottle.

As I got closer to Safeway, I started sweating, it felt like I had walked about ten miles, but really it was only about four, then there it was, YES! I had finally arrived. Now, despite my goal of getting Crown Royal, I ended up buying a bottle of Jack Daniels and the smallest bottle of Jägermeister. After all, it ended up being a few dollars less, and I felt like I got more. As soon as I left the Safeway, I walked a few more blocks, polishing off the Jack Daniels. I walked a little bit more, then called a cab to drive me back to my car. I briefly wondered what the hell I was doing drinking while waiting to get a ride to my car. Then, my psychotic brain took over; it tried to mathematically figure out how much I just drank, and the time I would have until the alcohol took effect, along with how much time I would need to drive without being impaired.

I then cracked open the Jägermeister and I chanted to myself, *Frank, you deserve this next buzz; besides, wouldn't you rather smell like black licorice than Jack Daniels.* I had about nine hours until I had to be to work, so I think we would all agree, I was outside the supposed eight-hour window of no alcohol before the next public task.

Once I got into the cab, I didn't drink. I wanted to be able to give the cabbie directions to my car ten miles away. I had to slow down on the sippin'—I didn't want to drive drunk; I had had enough trouble for now, right? The driver asked me a few verbal directions, and I helped him navigate to the liquor store where I was arrested. Ah, there it was: my car. I quickly tapped my pockets and ensured that I had the key. I paid the cabbie, got inside my car, buckled up, and took every back road I knew all the way home.

Once there, I kicked off my shoes, sat down, and yes, I had another drink to relax after a long, busy, trying day. I needed to wake up for work in about 5 ½ hours, so I only took another couple big swigs of Jäger.

Then I passed the fuck out.

Bzzz, Bzzz.

Bzzz, Bzzz.

With the alarm chiming, voila! It was morning. I ironed my clothes, jumped into the shower, and got super fly in my dark blue suit. It was a dark blue, pin-striped suit and I wore a light-blue button-up shirt with a power yellow tie. I was feeling myself at this point because I was looking way too good! I couldn't wait to get to work that day; I had an appointment at 1 o'clock, and I just knew that I could sell two more cars after that one. LET'S DO THIS!!

I reached inside my drawer where I always kept my keys. *Shit, where were my keys?* I reached into the freezer, took two more swigs of Jäger, and found my keys still in the deadbolt outside of my front door. I grabbed my shit, walked toward my car, buckled up, and off to work I went.

On my way out of the apartment complex, I realized that the powered security gate had almost hit my car. I thought to myself, hmm, that was odd because that hadn't happened before. Well, hello, of course, it didn't, I'm drunk, and I had pulled up to close to the gate, and when it swung open, it almost hit me! *Ah, fuck it, I'm out of here,* I thought, and off to work, I went.

Oh shit!

BANG... BANG... BANG... BANG... SMASH!

What the fuck was that? What just happened?

I awoke to a cop saying, "Sir? Sir, are you all right? Can you hear me? Sir, are you okay?" I thought to myself, oh my God, what happened?

I did a lot of blinking to clear my eyes, but beyond being next to my car and staring at my car driver's seat, I had no clue what was happening. I said I don't know. Why are you asking?

"Sir, you were in an accident, step over here behind the car and have a seat on the curb."

I said, ok, but can you tell me what happened again?

His name was Officer Melloch. He was joined at the scene soon after by Officer Lindh, who admonished me about taking the PAS test (Preliminary Alcohol Screening field test). At first, I declined, but I realized this whole thing wasn't going to end any better if I did not cooperate RIGHT NOW, so I agreed. He then had me blow into the breathalyzer.

"I need you to take a huge deep breath and blow into here."

Officer Lindh said, ". 325! And you are under arrest for driving under the influence!"

SHIT! Officer Melloch immediately grabbed me, cuffed me, and stuffed me in the back of the car in a way that suggested he was more than a little pissed off.

Now, I know what you all are thinking right now. "Frank, weren't you just arrested yesterday?" Uh… yes, that was me.

I'm in the squad car and *fuck, this sucks.* I felt like I was sobering up quickly, but seeing as how I blew a .325, I know that was just my mind playing tricks on me! Thoughts ran circles in my head.

Christina is going to kill me, and how the fuck am I going to be able to pick up my girls tonight? I don't even have a car—FUCK!! I'm never going to be allowed alone with the girls again.

There is nothing like the feeling of giving your ex-wife another upper hand on you.

Yeah, that was me, and so be it. I asked for it, all of it, right?

Once I arrived at the jail again, I couldn't stop thinking that I was just here last night. *What about work? What about my appointments? How am I going to sell three cars today? I am so fucked!* I was booked, fingerprinted, another yearbook photo was taken, and I was told to sit in the cell once again, but this time with a little more force.

While I was in the cell, it was as if I was in a *mitote*. To explain, in ancient times, the Toltecs spoke of the *mitote* as being in a fog-like state, very dreamy, and a state of mental confusion. This was me. A few more hours passed and I don't remember much of being in the cell because I was drunk and fell asleep, but when I regained consciousness I quickly stood up, patted myself, and gathered my senses. I was really sore and still felt a little confused. I noticed one of the policemen, recognizing him from Lauryn's school. He was one of the parents I would see when we got to play with the kids at recess and monitor their lunch periods. He recognized me as well.

"Hey, are you OK?" he asked.

I guess. I'm fine, but even more embarrassed now.

"At least you're OK. Let me check out for the day, and then I will see about getting you out. After that, I can pick you up outside on Taylor and go from there. Sound good?" he asked.

Cool, thank you, I said. I'll see you out there.

I felt both ashamed and relieved at the same time. Like the day before, I had to listen for my name, followed by my new favorite words: "Come with me." I went over to the counter and was given my belongings, then stood in line with about five or six others, just as I had twenty-four hours prior. When I finally walked out front, my police friend picked me up and gave me a ride home. During the trip, I shared with him what had happened and asked him his opinion on the whole thing.

He shrugged his shoulders and said, "Just tell the courts exactly how you remember it and what happened. Most of the time, your punishment can be reduced, but only if you tell the truth. It's when people try to lie that things get really messy, really quick."

(Here is a copy of the original police report taken on June 10, 2008)

STATE OF CALIFORNIA
NARRATIVE/SUPPLEMENTAL
CHP 556 (Rev. 7-90) OPI 061

Page 3 OF 3

DATE OF INCIDENT/OCCURRENCE	TIME	NCIC NUMBER	OFFICER I.D. NUMBER	NUMBER
6-10-08	1117	4313	3159	08 162 0459

☒ Narrative ☐ Supplemental
☐ Collision Report ☒ Other: DUI
☐ BA Update ☐ Hazardous Materials
☐ Fatal ☐ School Bus
☐ Hit and Run Update ☐ Other:

CITY/COUNTY/JUDICIAL DISTRICT
SAN JOSE / SANTA CLARA COUNTY / SAN JOSE MUNI

REPORTING DISTRICT/BEAT: WESTERN / N5   CITATION NUMBER

LOCATION/SUBJECT
DUI

STATE HIGHWAY RELATED ☐ Yes ☒ No

1. ON 6-10-08, AT 1117 HOURS, I WAS DISPATCHED TO A POSSIBLE
2. DUI CRASH. I ARRIVED AND (S) WAS STANDING NEXT TO HIS CAR.
3. (S) HAD JUST HIT 5 CARS. (S)'S CAR WAS IN THE ROADWAY WITH
4. MAJOR DAMAGE. I CONTACTED (S). (S) TOLD ME HE WAS THE
5. DRIVER AND THE VEHICLE BELONGED TO HIM.
6. (S) HAD BLOODSHOT WATERY EYES, SLURRED SPEECH, ODOR OF AN
7. ALCOHOLIC BEVERAGE, AND HAD PROBLEMS STANDING. (S) WAS
8. SWAYING AND HAD TO LEAN AGAINST A CAR TO KEEP FROM
9. FALLING.
10. (S) TOOK 3 FST'S. THE FIRST WAS THE FINGER DEXTERITY
11. TEST. (S) DID NOT FOLLOW DIRECTIONS AND KEPT COUNTING AFTER
12. THE TEST WAS OVER. (S) MISSED MANY FINGERS DURING COUNTING.
13. (S) COULD NOT KEEP HIS RIGHT RAISED LONGER THAN 5 SECONDS.
14. THE TEST REQUIRED A 9 SECOND LEG RAISED OFF THE
15. GROUND.
16. THE THIRD TEST WAS WALKING A STRAIT LINE ON THE
17. SIDEWALK. (S) KEPT FALLING OFF THE LINE. I TOLD (S) TO
18. ONLY WALK 9 STEPS. (S) KEPT GOING UNTIL I TOLD HIM TO
19. STOP. (S) HAD PROBLEMS ANSWERING QUESTIONS. I ASKED (S)
20. WHERE HE WAS. (S) DID NOT KNOW HIS LOCATION.
21. I ARRESTED (S) FOR DUI. (S) CHOSE A BLOOD TEST AT AIB.
22. I BOOKED (S) INTO JAIL.
23.
24.
25. ADDITIONAL INFO: OFFICER LINDH (2983) GAVE (S) A P.A.S. TEST. (S)
26. BLEW A .325.
27.
28.
29.
30.
31. ☐ Continued

PREPARER'S NAME and I.D. NUMBER	DATE	REVIEWER'S NAME	DATE
B. WOLFE 3159	6-10-08		

Use previous editions until depleted.

CHP 04 82767

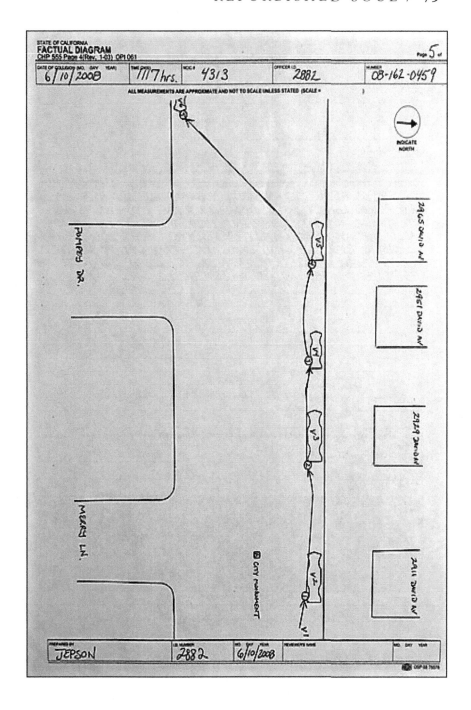

DMV
A Public Service Agency
COMPLETE IN BLACK INK

OFFICER'S STATEMENT
SECTIONS 13353 AND 13353.2 CVC

APS

LAW ENFORCEMENT AGENCY CASE NO.	ARREST DATE	FOR DMV USE ONLY				
08 162 0459	6-10-08					

DRIVER'S NAME (LAST, FIRST, M.I.)		DRIVER LICENSE NO	CLASS	STATE	THUMB PRINT (Right thumb or specify)
GARCIA, FRANK			C	CA	

MAILING ADDRESS ... STATE ZIP CODE

DOB: 11-23-69   Sex: M   Hair: BRN   Eyes: BRN   Ht: 5'9"   Wt: 185

Driver License: ☐ Suspended/Revoked ☒ Surrendered to Officer (Attach) ☐ Not in Possession ☐ Out-of-State
☒ 0.08% or more BAC Chemical Tests Results ☐ Chemical Test Refusal ☐ Forced Blood Test

PROBABLE CAUSE: (DESCRIBE IN DETAIL THE FACTS AND CIRCUMSTANCES THAT LED TO THE STOP OR CONTACT. COMPLETE AND SIGN THE CERTIFICATION BELOW.)

ON 6-10-08, AT 1117 HOURS, GARCIA CRASHED INTO 5 CARS WHICH WERE PARKED LEGALY ON THE ROADWAY. I CONTACTED GARCIA WHO WAS STANDING NEXT TO HIS CAR. GARCIA TOLD ME HE WAS THE DRIVER. GARCIA HAD BLOODSHOT WATERY EYES, SLURRED SPEECH, ODOR OF AN ALCOHOLIC BEVERAGE, AND COULD NOT STAND WITHOUT SWAYING. GARCIA BLEW A .325 P.A.S. GARCIA COULD NOT COMPLETE HIS FST'S. GARCIA DID NOT KNOW WHERE HE WAS.

I certify under penalty of perjury, under the laws of the State of California, that the information in the above statement is true and correct.

EXECUTED ON: Date 6-10-08 AT: City SAN JOSE County SANTA CLARA State CA

OFFICER'S PRINTED NAME	BADGE/ID/NO	SIGNATURE OFFICER
B. WOLFE	3759	X
AGENCY SJPD		AREA WESTERN

DS 367 (REV. 10/2005)   White—DMV   Yellow—Law Enforcement   Pink—Driver

When I finally got home, I sat there for about an hour before calling my boy Richie to share what had happened. I knew he would be a little disappointed. Then the call I really dreaded: I had to tell Christina what had happened.

She was disappointed and furious. That just added to my stress over the whole situation. Not only had I kept drinking when I knew I should have stopped, but now I had no car. I didn't know what to do next, and my anxiety was escalating rapidly. So, I did what I was now instinctively doing any time I wanted to numb my pain. If you recall, I hadn't finished the Jägermeister in the cab, so that fucker was still in my freezer. My twisted-up brain told me there was no better time than right now for a glass of Jägermeister over ice. That managed to chill me out a few notches, but I knew it wouldn't be enough to help me get some much-needed sleep. So, even though I was sore from the accidents, I walked to the liquor store, picked up some more Jäger, took a few sips as bedtime medicine, put the bottle in the fridge, and went to bed. I didn't know what the future held for me, and I was in no shape to make the future mine. About 6 weeks or so would pass, and I was in serious trouble mentally. I was scared and completely out of my mind. I'm not me, or was I?

The message was clear, and still, I didn't listen!

Angels' Roll Call -1

"**F**rankie, wake up. Hey! Hey, man. Frankie, wake up!*"* This is one of the toughest chapters to write; it's one of the hardest moments in my life to share. I was tired, done, and fed up; I had finally reached the conclusion that I had transformed into a failure, and that was now my future. I had nothing but failure to look forward to, and I was exhausted from looking at it.

I had failed at being a husband.

I had failed at being a father.

I had failed at being a good friend to many people.

I had failed at being a good employee.

I had failed at being the right child of God.

FUCK THIS, I'm out! I no longer want to live.

I had accepted these thoughts as my truth; no one could tell me differently. I was left with this one last thought: *get it done.* Be done with this life.

Despite the chilling reality, those thoughts actually gifted me a sense of warmth and security, almost like my mind was absolving me of my life's mistakes, bad decisions, and sinful ways. It was right at this time that I felt freedom from guilt, freedom from sadness, and freedom from all evil thoughts.

I had just—given—up.

In hindsight, it was the most selfish and utterly irresponsible thing I could do. I handed away all of life's blessings just like that. I just didn't want to *feel* anymore.

So, earlier that morning, I took five or six *oxy pills*, drank two fifth-size bottles of Crown, and finished what was left in a large bottle of Grey Goose. I remember looking toward the ceiling as the last drops of liquor hit my tongue.

I gagged a little, felt the burning of the alcohol across the roof of my mouth and throat; a couple of pills came back up, but I swallowed them again. There was nobody around, but I said "goodbye" anyway. My last thoughts before passing out were, "I hope this does it, and daddy loves you, girls."

The devil's antidote to love had taken charge of my every emotion. Bye!

"Frankie, wake up. Hey! Hey, man. Frankie, wake up! "

For it was only by the grace of God that I even came to. I woke to my co-worker's hand, nudging my shoulder, trying to shake me back to consciousness. I was face down on my living room floor, only wearing a pair of shorts. When I finally focused on what the hell was going on, I recognized my co-worker Joseph and my boy Richie. They both had been there for a bit, and thought I was dead! Well, so did I, well I supposed to be?

I was still way out of it and kept rubbing my head, trying to figure out why these guys were in my dream-like state, let alone my apartment. Minutes later, my apartment manager joined the group; she then said, "I feared that I had a dead person to deal with in my apartment complex and was glad to see you were alive." She had let them both in the front door.

Then December bursts into the apartment in tears; she couldn't stop crying and ran to hug me. Earlier when Richie told her he thought I was dead, she immediately fell apart, felt a sharp, empty pain of loneliness at the eternal loss of her best friend and confidant. She obviously was glad to see me alive as well.

Everyone in my living room seemed genuinely glad I was alive. But as for me, well, I was disappointed. As I managed to sit up onto my knees, all I could wonder was *why?* Why was I still here, breathing? Why wasn't I dead? Was I dreaming? Was this some kind of afterlife experience?

As soon as I sat up, everyone began to talk to me at once. It was a whirlwind of questions and concern; although I heard the words, I wasn't really making sense of anything. I don't remember what immediate questions they had—I can guess—and I don't have an understanding of what I voluntarily shared. Both Joe and Richie helped me struggle to my feet, but I couldn't stand up straight, I couldn't even hold any type of balance and made a quick beeline to sit on the couch.

Then, in walked Christina. Here I was, a guy who just tried to commit suicide, and all I could think was, she's going to *kill* me herself. I mumbled to her, hi Chris, and gave her a big hug.

She asked, "What is going on, Franklin?" The only answer I had was to shake my head. My eyes flooded with tears as I stared her in the face, she wanted a solution, and I wanted to give her one, but my lips just quivered to more tears coming down both of my cheeks. Everyone in my apartment began to sit on the couches as Chris helped me keep my balance, then assisted me to sit down. The room flooded with small talk, but I knew it was all an attempt to find out where I was physically, mentally, and emotionally.

Someone suggested that I really needed to get some help. After everything that led up to that moment, nothing could have sounded more comforting to my ears. I was burnt out, literally sick to death of being a drunken addict. I wanted relief. My sad attempt at an overdose—despite being the wrong solution—was a clear indication that I *needed* assistance, needed something different and needed help. In that second, I desperately wanted Christina to see me as something other than the complete mess in front of her. Something had to change, and it had to happen *now*.

I agreed to be taken to Good Samaritan Hospital, where I was assessed and was later checked into Mission Oaks (Good Sam's **psych** ward). During the intake process, I had an odd sense of belonging: I felt welcomed. The medical staff knew exactly what I needed and just how to approach the beginning of my recovery. It was quiet in there, and for a moment I felt like I was the lead character in a film about a crazy person.

What was I doing? Was this right for me? What was Christina going to do? What was she going to think of me? Was she going to have an advantage between the girls and me once again? I needed these thoughts to STOP ringing through my head. I had no drugs and no alcohol in there to dim the pain. Things just got more real!

A few hours later, I was regaining my senses in my room when a knock at the door signaled the arrival of the ward psychiatrist, an older woman with lots of grays, just like in the movies. As we talked, I quickly realized this wasn't a personal interview for me but was instead a generic psych ward evaluation to see where I was emotionally and if I was mentally sound.

She was the textbook definition of cold and clinical; she spoke more to her paperwork than to me. I wasn't in a position to be critical about her bedside manner, so I let her do her thing. What she lacked in personal warmth, she made up for in relief at the end of her evaluation. She prescribed meds for my common withdrawal symptoms that were clearly obvious to her; I had been shaking like leaves on a tree during a storm. After she left, I lay back down and gazed at the ceiling. I still wasn't one hundred percent yet, I needed the drugs and booze to wear off, so I closed my eyes in an attempt to sleep it all away.

Within a half-hour or so, I heard loud squeaky rollers coming down the hall. The nurse knocked at the door and said: "Dinner's ready if you are up to it." I took her up on the offer, washed my face and hands, and headed out. As I walked down the hallway, there were large stainless-steel bins filled with warm food. I waited in the small line and asked just above my regular voice if anyone had any Jack Daniels to go with dinner; a few of the others laughed, and a couple of people replied with "Right, and no shit, hah."

After I got my dinner tray, I looked for a place to sit. After sitting down alone, a single thought popped into my mind: *I need a drink.* Now, I know it sounds whack after the events of that morning had put me in there, but that's how I felt. I also learned that the other addicts and alcoholics around me shared similar pangs. I'd just have to learn to deal with them.

The next morning came crashing onto my head as I woke up feeling like shit. My body felt like it weighed over 300 pounds. Everything I did was in slow-motion. My head pounded. My body ached. I was groggy and had a slight case of diarrhea. If you haven't guessed, it didn't feel like a day at summer camp. As I dried off after a long shower, I heard the squeaky roller sound again.

But now I associated it with a warm meal heading my way. When you're going through withdrawal, your appetite swells, so I washed my face and hands, grabbed my meds, and swiftly headed to breakfast.

I picked up my tray and found a seat. It was my first experience of sitting with others who also needed help, as I didn't get a chance to meet most of them the previous night. To my surprise, within two minutes of sitting, there was a sudden and incredible frenzy at the table. It wasn't fighting or misbehaving—it was trading time! What the hell? Apparently, a regular feature of mealtime is that everyone at the table starts bartering and marketing different breakfast foods that we didn't want for the foods that we did want. I also learned that we had a specific contact for "real coffee" other than decaf, that is. Yep, even the psych ward had, you guessed it, a "coffee guy"!

My mealtime education continued as a woman sitting next to me introduced herself and everyone else at the table. She also explained the daily regimen to me; basically, 100% of our time was pre-scheduled, and not really optional. This is how it looked.

> » Breakfast—Group session—Arts & crafts—Alone time.
> » Lunch—Group session—Self-improvement projects—Alone time.
> » Dinner—Group session—Free time.
> » Bedtime.

Rinse, Repeat. Day after day.

During my time at Mission Oaks, I became more aware of who I was and confirmed who I no longer wanted to be. Coping with detox from one addictive substance was horrible, let alone having to go through two at the same time. Man, I was hurting all over, but eventually, it became a little easier. I spent a lot of time wondering what had happened to me, and how could I have gotten to this point. I was without love, without God, and my trapezius muscles were sore from the devil's cords pulling so hard.

As more time went on, it helped that the ward had specific visiting hours, and the essential people in my life could come by. December came to see me as often as she could. I missed her dearly, and she had witnessed quite a bit thus far, yet had the strength to allow me her love. Christina also made it a point to bring the girls in when she could, and I cherished those precious minutes with them. Lauryn's little face would light up, and she would hug me so tight. To this day, I can still hear her soft little voice tell me, "Hi, and I love you, daddy." Ysabella with her beautiful little self would do the same shortly after her big sis. Ahh, their little voices, those soft little voices would play a significant role within me later.

While at Mission Oaks, I taught myself to present the "real" me, something I rarely could do when I was under the influence and making up elaborate excuses for almost every occasion. I didn't have the energy to muster up another story for either Christina or December; more than that, I finally realized that I *didn't want to* lie to these key women in my life. I am genuinely grateful for December who help me cope, and she will forever have a spot within my heart. I know Christina had to fight emotionally to make the trips to see me. After all, I was the guy that hurt her. One side of her had to be thinking, "Well, he deserves it!" But she worked through those thoughts and had a sophisticated understanding to know that time with my daughters would assist the healing process within me. Christina knew that I needed to hold my girls, to kiss my girls, to see my girls, and after that, the rest of that day would be better.

Thank you again, Christina!

By the time ten days had gone by at Mission Oaks, I was getting restless. I felt like pursuing *more* help in my recovery. But everything I had heard from others indicated that most recovery centers were far away, and recovery lasted about a month. I had already taken off many days from work, so I first reached out to my co-worker to see if it would even be possible to keep my job if I left for an extended period. I also asked Christina if she could hold things down for me with the girls if I were gone for several weeks. I ran the scenario by Richie and December to ensure they would have my back while I was gone.

Everyone was more than receptive. With everyone's support, I began reaching out to a few recovery centers and learning about my options. My first lesson was a shock: it would cost me tens of thousands of dollars just to show up at their doorstep. I mean, where would I get that kind of money? Plus, even if I had that kind of cash, my first instinct would be to give it to Chris and my girls. I worried that I had already reached a dead end.

But sometimes life can give you *good* news (a surprise, right?) and I soon discovered that my medical benefits would cover my stay at a licensed center. After further research, I chose Camp Recovery Center in Scotts Valley because they made me feel the most comfortable during the initial phone conversation. From that moment, my mind was set, and I made the Camp Recovery Center my new mission in life.

On August 28, 2008—15 days after admission to Mission Oaks—it was time to go. I made my bed military-style one more time, gathered my belongings, and checked myself out. A few minutes later, my boy Richie swooped in, picked me up, and off we went, heading south on Highway 17 to Scotts Valley. I felt great for the first time in a long time with the wind in my face and the sun in my eyes through the sunroof. I was free, free to breathe, and free from substances. We made record time through the Santa Cruz Mountains, and just 15 miles later we arrived at the Camp Recovery Center. Richie parked his car, popped his trunk, gave me a hug, and off I went.

Thanks, Richie. I love you, man!

I went up to the intake door, knocked, and introduced myself to the on-duty intake person. She was kind, warm, and tried to relate to me by telling me her boyfriend was in the military. We went over all of the paperwork, and I learned that my benefits would cover all but about $5,500 of my visit. I paused for a few minutes, called Richie to get his opinion, and he said he would cover me if I couldn't repay it after the allotted time from my projected release date. I finished all the paperwork and headed for lunch. Oh, damn, the cafeteria was top notch. I grabbed a tray, plate, bowl, and silverware and started to order my food from the cook. What, no metal bins with warmed food? No. There were several choices, and it seemed like the food was plentiful. After eating just about all my stomach could handle, I headed up to my cabin. The camp was set up with cabins lined up along a trail in the woods, separated by about twenty to thirty yards. The men were separated from the woman, but if you were there long enough, most knew you couldn't keep us divided.

Anyway, let's move on. If you recall, I already did my detox at Mission Oaks, and there were some people here who had not even begun to detox yet. You could plainly see those who were not feeling good and those who were. After I unpacked my clothes, I headed to the first-afternoon activity outdoors. You could play frisbee, tennis, go for a walk (but not too far or alone), or you could lift weights. I went swimming that afternoon and just tried to calm my anxiety down. I tried so hard to focus on my recovery, but real life never really goes away, and all you can do is prolong its issues. After I went swimming, I joined this outside group session, which was reviewing what they had done so far in recovery and what they were looking to do in recovery. It was here that I nicknamed myself *Vincent Vega* as in from the movie *Pulp Fiction*. I loved that movie, and I loved Vincent's character.

My first day would end as follows, I ate dinner, went to a final group meeting, and then to bed. The first night was tough; I was in a different world then I was used to at Mission Oaks; I was out in the woods, and the poor guy who slept next to me was tremoring and screaming due to his own body detoxing. As the moon glared through the window, I could see he was moving around uncontrollably, and I know what his body was screaming to do. I will admit that even while at this moment while watching him, I too wanted to get high just one more time. Needless to say, I didn't sleep that much, and nor could he.

As the next day dawned, I got up, brushed my teeth, and headed to breakfast. After I ate, I went and talked to my new counselor. She would have the high duty of helping me-*Vincent Vega* get healed. Yeah, right, maybe not healed, but at least better. My camp time progressed, and most days consisted of breakfast, group, socializing, alone time, lunch, group, socializing, alone time, dinner, group, and go to bed. On the weekends' if you were good, you were allowed to have a visitor come. I had my close friends Richie and Danielle come and see me one Sunday. I was so happy to see them, and we spent about an hour together. They both reassured me that life on the outside was of no worry to me and that they just wanted the old FG back. I completed my four weeks of recovery with gusto; I not only felt better physically, but I felt mentally healthy as well. I was focused, rejuvenated, and was ready for anything life could throw at me!

Except, how could I forget that I still had all of my DUI bullshit waiting for me when I got out. The day I checked out, and Richie picked me up, was as if I hit a fifty-foot wall, BOOM! Reality.

I was still facing repercussions from my two arrests; thank God for my lawyer Mr. Kelly, who was also in the family. While I was at camp, Mr. Kelly handled much of my mess for me and took care of the bulk of the DMV side of things. Man, I love that guy. I felt as if I could face anything with Mr. Kelly by my side.

As to the actual charges I was facing—I got the "drunk in public" from the liquor store dismissed, then pleaded "no contest" to the misdemeanor DUI. There were hefty fines, a lot of Sunday work-days, and nine months of DUI School. And like a dumbass, I actually had to restart the DUI School over during my third month because I dropped out. Why, why did I drop out? You probably guessed it: I went to one of my classes high and buzzed, and at that very moment, I at least had enough sense to quickly head for the restroom, and since I didn't want to get busted, I quit. Of course, that cost even more money, but given the circumstances, I could have gotten in more severe trouble.

Now, if anyone of you has ever done or been to DUI classes, then you know that nine months is a long time, but I deserved every minute of it because we all know that on the morning of my DUI, I could have easily hurt or even killed someone. I blew a .325 and hit 4 cars, remember?

Thank you, Mr. Kelly, and I apologize, sir.

The message was clear and, in my face, but I still didn't listen.

The Interim, Part Two

During the next few months, I, unfortunately, refreshed my acquaintance with the interim. Yes, that deep, dark state of mental anguish, where if one isn't careful, you could wind up mentally insane or worse, dead. It was an emotionally unsafe place that I hated; it was everyday life in total limbo. It is where I would just drift around in this mental fog until that next big thing, job, relationship, promotion, diet, or even a new look. All the while, I knew it was total destruction waiting to happen. You see, if you do not remain on the right course, the interim can and will take you down—first in thought, then in action. It's that powerful.

I was on cloud nine when I left rehab, and I was enjoying my life for the first time since I could remember. I left the camp on September 28, 2008, and managed to handle all of my court issues without lying and without fail. I was determined to stay on the straight and narrow. Besides, I was Frank Garcia, and you would need an army to bring me down, at least in thought.

I'd like to say I couldn't have foreseen what happened next in any lifetime. But the truth is: I could have and should have. As most would say, history does repeat itself.

A couple of months later, for my birthday in November, I decided to thank myself for staying sober for nearly 4 months, so I did it, I bought a mini bottle of that tasty black licorice (you know, Jägermeister). I know, that seems like a fly in the face after everything I had just experienced, but I approached this situation methodically, and with caution. The "good" side of my brain screamed an on-going series of "no's," but the wrong-thinking side of my mind had "logical" responses. "Frank, it's just a small celebration," whispered the voice inside. "You're in full control. It's only a mini bottle. You know you can handle wa-a-a-y more than that. Besides, no one will ever find out." Who was I to argue with such logic?

So, I did it. Yep, I drank the mini, and I maintained my control to only drink that one. No harm, no foul? Good job, me! I've made it! Right?

Wrong!!

I not only survived my birthday but Thanksgiving and Christmas as well. I told myself, "You got this! You're in control!" But as much as I deluded myself, I was full-on *not ready* for the next big holiday. Welcome to New Year's Eve 2008/9 and a very moody ex-wife. Me, still feeling confident in my ability to maintain control, I reached out to Christina and asked if the girls could come to stay with me for New Year's while she went out. It seemed like a win-win for everyone. Right?

That… was the wrong fucking thing to ask her.

"The girls are with me," Christina replied angrily. "The girls won't be with you on New Year's, EVER!" Click!

Really?

Well *fuck it then*, I sternly said out loud. If I can't have the two biggest joys in my life tonight, I'm drinking! Where are my keys?

After all, this was my fight, and why did I need to care about Christina or what she had to say? It's drinks on me! So, I put on some cool gear and went to Richie's to meet up with some friends. I was safe there, and I knew I wouldn't be judged by anyone. I welcomed 2009 in with quite a buzz, and in slow fashion on my way to a higher state of drunkenness. My body felt as if I had never even stopped.

Yes! This is it; I was King of the Moment! Fuck the world and anyone against me! Yet, as it always did, this lifestyle would once again prove who was in charge… (Hint: it wasn't me.)

The message was clear, and yet, I still didn't listen.

Where's my blanky?

Blanky, you ask? Umm, yes, I still have my favorite blanket, and no, not the one from when I was a child. I still have the blanket from my drinking days. It is gray, it looks like a modern-day knit style, and I don't believe I have washed it since I quit. Who cares, it's mine, and it really means a lot to me. I even remember once my girlfriend asking me if WE can throw it away. To which I said, WHAT! WE? Um no, and never! I told her you have no idea what this blanket and I have been through.

Now, I will say, she did know about the relationship I had with my falling apart *Rip Curl* beach sandals. Yes, I still have those as well; they were my drinking sandals and more about them later. I seriously doubt that I am the only alcoholic out there that still clings to unique clothing or other items that remind us of our pursuit of the lonesome drunk or high state. But, during my days of alcoholic madness, I would often correlate my drunken state with being warm and cozy in my blanky. It was like both went hand in hand. For example, comfort to me was to get some good liquor, go home, put on my comfy clothes, make sure the door is locked, caress my bottle, and cozy up with my blanky. At the time, I didn't feel I was at home until her gentle cotton touch caressed my body, and my lady Crown Royal in her beautiful velvet dress soothes the inner walls of my throat.

My blanky was it for me. It took me into the land of the wilderness where I can roam the woods.— I loved to drink and watch MTV allowing Ms. Crown to do her thing with my brain. She was wild, and she knew just how I liked her, out of her velvet dress, top off, and slowly dripping across my lips. I knew as blanky did, that deep down she came in second to me, but I only really distanced her when I would have Lauryn and Ysabella over to visit. I would talk to blanky before the girls came over, and I would gently say: look, it's all about you and me, but you must remember while my girls are here, you have to stay quiet and put away. Please, I said as I folded and tucked her away in the closet.

Yes, blanky always tried to make her way in between my girls and I. Upon hearing her question for a second time I would say; look blanky, I am sorry, but my girls are most important and besides I have bought them their own blankies, Yes, even a blanket has its way of conversing with you through its displeasure.

Night after night blanky, and I would fall asleep together or should I say pass out. And the next thing you know, we would also come too together. I rarely say wake up because waking up isn't what I did, I only came too out of a deep state of drunkenness. My time with blanky was a sad and dark time for me. I could *Jump Around* to the *House of Pain*. I would sing *Big Girls Don't Cry* with *Fergie*, and dance with *Bruno Mars* as he sang *Nothin on You*.

Oh, yea, I mentioned my beach sandals earlier, and those too meant a lot to me. I wore my beach sandals everywhere. I would slip them on in the early morning around 0530, so I could walk to the closest liquor store that opened its doors at 0600. I wore my beach sandals anytime I would roam the streets of Campbell or San Jose. No matter where I was, there they were too. Funny thing is, sometimes I would have to lose them temporarily by throwing them in the nearest bushes because I would take off running from the Police. Yes, I would be walking and notice a cop pass by me in my buzzed to drunken state of mind. I would see them through my glazed eyes and instantly become paranoid, and think they saw me drunk. I would monitor if they were turning around, and sometimes they would, and I was off to the races. I was hauling ass so I wouldn't get a drunk in public; hence arrested again. Then I would wait for hours to go back and look for my beach sandals that I threw in someone's bushes. Usually, as I was rummaging through the bushes, the homeowners would yell out, "Hey, you get out of there!" And to them, I would say, I'm sorry, Sir or ma'am, but earlier on my walk, my keys flew out of my hand when I sneezed. I know you are all probably thinking, shit did that work? Yes, it did, every time. I loved those sandals. I loved the support they gave me, and I loved the fact that no matter what I was going through, they were too.

My sandals even went with me on my 28-day vacation in the mountains. But like most things, they too came to an end. I was walking down the stairs one day, slightly tripped, and I started to recover my footing, but my foot went through the toe splitter of the sandal. I still have them, and I'm thinking of having them bronzed, crazy right?

Thank you, Officer X,

On this day, I woke up starving, but first, I needed my fix of liquor but my then-favorite taqueria off of Bascom Ave. wasn't open yet. This day was like any other day in summer, a little warm and very bright outside. I started drinking about 0600, and this I know because I opened the liquor store with the employee on Hamilton Ave. I drank all the way back to my apartment, and for whatever reason, I couldn't wrap my mind around what my life had become. It was filled with thoughts of emptiness, sadness, and I was physically drained. After I got back to my apartment, I tried to relax and not focus too much on what I had become, but to just enjoy my next escape from reality and function. Man, a quesadilla, and a couple of tacos sure sound good.

I waited a couple of hours and called in sick. The fact of the matter is that I was not well mentally. I grabbed my blanky and lay on the couch and put MTV on hoping to see some fresh videos. I continued drinking while I waited for the taqueria to open. About a half-hour went by, and wouldn't you know it? There she was, Fergie came on and was either singing to or with me, and I don't remember that minute part, but I loved her voice. After my time with Fergie passed,

I felt the Interim begin to proxy in suicide again as if it was the thing to do. I don't even know where this came from, yet it was ready to pounce on me like a Lion to a Gazelle. It was at this time that I needed to run, I knew what the Interim's power had and what it could do to me. But no, I didn't have enough deposited in my spiritual account to handle this, not at this time.

Unfortunately, the darkness had a hold of me, and I couldn't get out of its way quick enough, along with its thoughts of suicide once again raining on my drunken utopia. I began to stare at the knife on the counter, contemplating slitting my wrists or drinking more so I could put a knife in my chest. I don't know why the mess of blood all over, or staining the carpet, was even a thought at this moment, but it was. I went over to my desk, and even while slipping into a deeper state of drunkenness, I reviewed my life insurance policy to make sure that it included suicide as a way of death coverage, and it did. The further truth is, that is one of the prerequisites for me obtaining the insurance in the first place.

In the end, I just wanted the three most important girls in my life to receive the monetary benefit. After reading the documents, I went over and propped myself up onto the kitchen counter next to the wooden knife set. Now I was thinking; do I go with the large ones or the smaller thinner one? I took out the medium size knife instead, and I proceeded to cut just the first layer of the epidermis on my chest just over my heart. I carved an "X" only into the top layer of my skin and smeared the blood across my chest with the knife's edge. I then poked a small hole into my wrist as if to say to myself, ok, which one is it going to be. I now had two areas of bleeding, and my mind growing numb. I don't remember feeling scared. I would say that I was in a calmer place absolutely due to the alcohol. I set the knife down, went to the restroom to watch the blood running down my chest and wrist. I looked in the mirror in acknowledgment that I indeed found the right spot, my chest.

Next, I remember feeling like I had switched thought-spaces, and for whatever reason, I noticed enough time had passed, and I still wanted to go to the taqueria, so I did. I grabbed my famous rip curl sandals, and off I went. As I walked across the Hamilton Bridge over highway 17, I thought things would be much easier if I just jumped onto the freeway, it was a short thought, and I continued to walk on.

I arrived at the taqueria, ordered my food, and I drank a few more beers. After I finished everything, I began to walk back to my apartment. There I was again getting closer to the highway 17 bridge. This time it was on, there was no time for second-guessing. I paused, waited for the light to be green so there was no stopped traffic on the bridge. I climbed up onto the fence, got as high as I could, and without further thought, I tried to throw my feet up over the top. I wanted to make this quick, but I missed and fell back down onto the pavement.

The next thing I knew, I was woken up by an officer, I don't remember from what department, I just remember being asked if I was ok and what happened. He then helped me into a police car. I was asked where I lived, and I told him just right over there behind the Elephant Bar, as I pointed. This kind officer gave me ride home when he really could have charged me with drunk in public, or taken me to a hospital for attempted suicide. A possible 51/50 hold, again. Maybe he didn't have enough information, perhaps he really didn't see all that had happened, who knows, and perhaps he was God sent. Nonetheless, to him, I say thank you, Officer X, for not doing what you could have, but for getting me home and allowing me another chance to repair my *refurbished soul*.

This message too was clear, and again, I didn't listen.

SCENE XIII

Lost 'n' Found

The flight attendant was pleasant, sexy, and cheerful. As she took notice of my seat assignment, she then looked me in the eye and softly said, "Hi, and good evening. Is there anything we can get for you?"

Good evening, I said, I'll have four bottles of Crown Royal and a Coke, please.

Her slightly shocked expression spoke volumes. "I'm sorry sir, did you say four?"

Yes, please and thank you in advance, I get a little anxious while flying and I don't want to have to bother you again. To which she then said, "Hmm, ok, I understand and let me see what I can do, I'll be right back."

My seat assignment was in the middle seat of Flight 606 from San Francisco straight into Amsterdam. As the flight attendant returned, she said, "Here you go, sir, four bottles of Crown Royal and one coke." I said thank you and immediately lined up all four bottles in some-odd OCD way. It was much like how a drill instructor would line up his recruits and grill them. For me, I only had one in-your-face question for these four bottles of Crown: Are you worthy of me jumping off the wagon and tossing you back into my body? Stand up straight, you little Crown soldiers, I am talking to all of you!

As I sat and considered drinking these four bottles with eager anticipation, there was a fierce tug-of-war going on in my brain. If you'll remember from previous scenes, these voices and how they chant to me become all too real, and therefore the all-too-familiar argument between good and evil ensues.

Voice 1 calmly suggested, "Frank, you got this. It's only four, and you can just stop again when you're done, or after we have landed on solid ground."

Voice 2 pleaded, "Frank, you are so much stronger than this! Please don't drink them, please."

I glanced at my watch, and I was facing a flight of more than 12-hours still ahead of me; that's a long time, and besides, there would be plenty of time for the alcohol to wear off. That's it, no one will know, here we go. Fuck off, Voice 2. I'm getting in this.

I cracked the first seal and could feel the saliva already gathering under my tongue. I grabbed the plastic cup and slowly poured the amber liquid over the ice. *Ah, who needs Coke in this? Besides, that's not how one should enjoy a Crown Royal.*

I emptied the bottle, put the lid back on, and set it to the side. I told myself that it really didn't count as "drinking" when you're 36,000 feet in the air. I was officially on an international flight and not on the ground. My alcoholic mind made whatever excuses and advance damage control it could to ensure that the first sip went down guilt-free. It felt like the first time I was with a woman and discovered *oh, hot damn! Yes, I'm a FREAK!*

I wasted no time finishing that first mini bottle of liquor and began to pour the second, quickly adding a dash of Coke. I convinced myself that if I downed this next drink fast enough, the smart side of my brain wouldn't have time to coach me otherwise.

You be quiet, Voice 2! This second drink also went down nice and smooth (and yes, each bottle was set back into formation and at attention, awaiting my next order). This time I was the drill instructor, and they needed to listen.

Before my next drink, I reached up into the overhead compartment and grabbed my homework for the business class I was taking; I wanted to make sure I completed my assignment before we landed. Psshh, yeah, right. That never happened, and to this day, I still don't even know what happened to my hundreds of dollars in school books tucked away in my black Louis Vuitton bag that I left in the overhead bins (I know, I know, but the bag was a gift). Yep, all gone. Instead, I slipped on my headphones and felt like it was time to get my party on! I bought all the people around me a drink and we all began to shoot the shit. The drinks kept coming and soon enough, all my little mini liquor soldiers were at attention, yet sadly empty.

I looked up to get my flight attendant's attention but stopped; I was afraid she might say no. So instead, I watched her walk away. When I felt she was far enough, I grabbed the attention of a nearby male attendant.

I asked, may I please have—

"—Four bottles of Crown Royal, sir?" Oh shit! He finished my sentence.

I paused for a second. *How did he know that? Never mind, it doesn't matter.* Yes, I confirmed. And 1 Coke with ice, please.

Nothing else was said but I'm sure he knew I already had enough because he only brought me two bottles with the Coke. I socialized a little more and began to enjoy the next two bottles. By this time, I told myself I'd better lay off, so I'd be OK once we landed in Amsterdam. I requested a set of the airline's headphones for the onboard movie and finished my drinks. Man, I-was-drunk! I asked for a couple of pillows and a blanket, knowing that if I fell asleep quickly that I would have time to shake off these drinks.

Later, I was awakened by the attendant and asked if I wanted a blanket and a pillow. *What?* Confused, I looked around. I definitely didn't have pillows or a blanket anymore. Maybe I'd handed them to my neighbors? Anyway, I said yes and fell back asleep.

Sleep didn't last long, though, and I awoke to feeling hungry. By this point, it had been several days since I'd really eaten anything. I ordered a pesto pasta dish that turned out to be really tasty, plus more of that bread and butter that came with it.

Halfway through my meal, a cart pulled up next to me, and a soft voice asked, "Would you like a glass of wine with your dinner, sir?"

What? Wine? And it was free? *Oh, hell yeah.* You don't have to ask an alcoholic twice! I said, sure! Now, you may be thinking that it's not a smart move to mix hard liquor and wine. But, hello, it was *free*! That's what we alcoholics do!

I finished the pesto pasta and slowly sipped my wine. A few hours went by, where I lost track of everything and dropped back into slumber. Eventually, there was a tap on my shoulder, along with a firm voice that told me to fasten my seatbelt for landing. I awoke suddenly, frazzled, and in a panic.

OH SHIT!! Where am I? OK, OK, hold on, Frank. I knew I had to pull this together and *fast*! I said I had to use the bathroom, and against their wishes, ran to the back of the plane to rinse my face and clean myself up as best I could. Splash, splash, my hands threw water onto my face. *You got this, Frank. You got this!* I went back to my seat, buckled up, and stared across the aisle out the window as we approached Amsterdam International Airport. Then out of nowhere, I was hit with overwhelming anxiety, worse than any I had felt before. I thought it was just because I was overseas, so I kept pushing forward, with a white-knuckled grip on the armrests of my seat. I let go, and *Here we go!*

As soon as I got off of the plane, I found the closest counter to ask about my connecting flight to Munich. The attendant gave me a concerned look and asked if I was OK? I said, um yes, I am, why? She then shook her head as if to say, yeah, right. Within seconds, she found the connecting gate number of my flight. She then said it was a fair distance away, so I would have to hurry to catch it. I thanked her and rushed off. I had had enough time for the alcohol to wear off, but I felt lethargic, and I didn't hurry quick enough, so I missed my connecting flight to Munich.

What now? I won this trip, it was for my job, and I needed to get to Munich ASAP! While at the counter, I asked, how soon can I get the next flight to Munich. No luck there; I was looking at either a pretty long wait, or I could pay a significantly large amount to fly on an alternate airline. There was no way I could pay the amount they were asking; I just didn't have that kind of money.

I stepped away from the counter and asked this one guy for the fastest way to Munich besides flying. He said the train and pointed in the general direction of the train station. I was desperate and needed to do whatever it took to get to Munich as soon as possible...

At this point, I was completely sober, and although I didn't feel well, I was just glad to be on the ground and coherent.

I walked outside of the airport and was instantly struck by how beautiful it was. Despite my situation, I felt pretty optimistic and very lucky to be there. I walked down the sidewalk in the direction I believed led to the train station. As I looked for a taxi to flag down, a guy walked up to me. At first, I thought he was going to try and help by giving me directions. Wrong! As we started to talk, and through the outer corner of my eye, I saw him motion another guy to come over. He attempted to regain my attention by mumbling some directions. I tried to pay attention even though I was still aware of the other guy coming toward us, and HOLY SHIT! WHAT THE FUCK!

The second guy rushed me with a big piece of wood about a yard long while the first guy tried to pull my bag off from across my body. With my left forearm, I was able to quickly block the wood from hitting my head; man, that fuckin' *hurt*. The first guy struggled to get my bag off, and I kept punching the second guy on the side of the face while I held his shirt close to me. Unfortunately, the first guy finally managed to get away with the iPod I had in my front pocket. He then took off while I continued to fight the second guy. It was on; I was *not* losing this battle. People gathered as we kept at it, but what the hell, no one wanted to get involved. I kept swinging, swinging hard. I mean, I was swinging all the way from Cleveland! I knew that no matter how this ended, we'd both be hurting later.

He kept trying to get my wallet and pull off my leather bag. But there was no way I was giving in! I continued to do what I knew best: defend Frank and make every swing count! After what seemed like forever, I finally fended off the second guy, and he took off. Maybe he thought the American was just going to give in, but hell no! Not *this* Cali- boy.

Feeling somewhat safe with the crowd nearby, I checked to see what I'd lost. I managed to hang on to my bag, wallet, watch, and headphones, but the first guy for sure got away with the iPod. I was pissed, it was fairly new, and I had a ton of songs on it, but still very grateful to be alive even with a severely bruised forearm where the wood struck me. *What the hell?* Better my arm than my face or head, right? Funny enough, I remember thinking at the time that my instructor Mike Velasquez from Fight Factory in San Jose would have been proud of me. Man, I liked Mike... and what he taught me probably saved me from a beating. Thanks, Mike.

I needed a moment alone to assess all that had happened and make a plan to get to Munich, so I went to a nearby pub. Wouldn't you know it, in Amsterdam, you can drink in public. *Uh-oh.* I ordered a large, cold beer and grabbed a seat on a nearby bench. The adrenalin started to wear off, and I was beginning to feel sore. My arm and ribs hurt like hell, my shirt was torn up, and I was missing one of my sleeves. A few pints later, picking at one of my bloody knuckles, I wondered how I was still going to get to Munich… and why was I drinking in public?

I continued in the direction that I thought led to the train station. By this point, I really needed to use the restroom. I came across this beautiful hotel and headed inside to find some relief. I was immediately approached by some guard who saw me come in, and he asked me to leave. My first thought was I did not want any more trouble, so I turned to leave. But the alcohol, which had a tendency to arouse an angry side of me, just couldn't leave things alone. I let that guard have it with some good ol' American curse words; he had a few of his own as well. Ah, it's not worth it, I thought to myself.

I kept it moving. Here I was again, walking around semi-drunk in the streets of Amsterdam, just like I had done in San Jose, Campbell, and Los Gatos.

Holy SHIT!! Why am I cuffed to this hospital bed? I didn't even remember how I got here, let alone wake up here. I quickly regained consciousness and sat up.

What's going on? I asked.

A nurse with warm hands said, "Hello, Frank. You are at VU Medisch Centrum."

(In English: You're at the VU University Medical Center in Amsterdam.)

After looking at my check-in sheet, I figured it out pretty quick: I was drunk, the local police had found me on the sidewalk and brought me in. And just so I had clarity, I asked the nurse why I was brought here?

She told me, "The police brought you in because you were lying across the sidewalk complaining of pain. They could see by the looks of your arm, knuckles and torn clothes that you had been in some trouble, the cuffs were only for your safety."

Who does this? Well, an alcoholic does. So, there I was, lying in bed, cuffed, drunk, and in a lot of pain from my forearm up to my shoulder. The doctors and nurses were all very kind, speaking to me with their cool accents. I then realized that I was drunk in a hospital overseas, and that is *not* cool. I finally succumbed to the exhaustion after my eventful day and drifted into a nap.

I awoke later with the nurse's warm hands again on my wrist, checking for my pulse. She asked me how I was feeling, and with no warning, my eyes flooded with tears. Yes, at that moment I couldn't hold it in, I was past making up stories. I blurted out that I was an alcoholic-addict from America and I needed to get to Munich. She gripped my hand in a comforting way, moved a little closer, and said, "It will be okay, Garcia."

The doctor returned and she conferred with him. He sent her to get me some meds, which helped me fall back asleep. Morning came and when I awoke the next time, I immediately asked if I could check myself out. By now, they were happy to assist me. After all, who wanted to keep the drunken American taking up a bed, right? The doctor gave me a few meds to go, told me how and when to take them. I left the hospital in Amsterdam and continued on my trek to Munich.

heelkunde

spoedeisende hulp

De Boelelaan 1117   postbus 7057   telefoon 020 444 3636   www.vumc.nl
1081 HV Amsterdam   1007 MB Amsterdam   fax 020 444 3510   heelk@vumc.nl

GARCIA
Frank

2 68 76 93
BSN:
23-11-1969 M
EH
(000)/

Us
EIGENR
Huisarts: Onbekend
11-02-2011 14:07

VU university medical center

Dear Colleague,

On February 11 -2011 Your Patient: Mr Garcia, Frank

visited our casualty ward because of:

Physical examination: Pt did not wake up when was spoken to. Smells of ethanol. No neurological abnormalities. RR 110/62 Hf 60 saturation 100%

X-ray:

Laboratory findings: glucose 6, ethanol 3.9 G/L other findings all normal. Tox screening: NEGATIVE

ECG: normal

Additional research or specialistic care:

Diagnosis: Ethanol intoxication

Therapy: thiamine 100mg IV / observation vital parameters Iv NaCl 0.9% 1Lt. catheterisation

Advise for further treatment:

Yours sincerely, E Vanderwater
Emergency Physician

By now, I knew I had to call my boss. But what would I say? That I got lost? Yeah, right. Well, it wasn't exactly a lie because I really was lost, but within my soul. I found a phone and called back to the states. I told my boss that I was okay, a little lost, but that I was still heading to Munich by train. To this day, I can still remember hearing everything in my boss's voice that he didn't say outright; I knew that he really cared about me, but he was beyond tired of my shit. Besides, I was only one employee, and he had many to worry about.

I hung up, wandered off, and stopped at a pub about two miles down from the hospital to grab some food and maybe a drink or two. I popped a pill that I was given for my pain and washed it down with a glass of whiskey. Yes, I knew it was wrong for me to do, but it's just what we substance abusers do! I continued to drink for the rest of the day. I had to, man; it was quite an adventurous twenty-four hours.

I wandered around Amsterdam all day, semi sightseeing, and stupidly drinking.

Nightfall donned and I came across a patch of soft grass about 200 feet from the main street, laid down, and fell asleep. I slept through the night. When I woke up, I discovered some kind soul had actually given me some sort of blanket to cover with.

Now that I was awake, I headed for the closest pub for some much-needed food and drink. As I finished breakfast, I reconfirmed my next mission: head for the train station at all costs. As I walked around looking for the station, I realized I was seeing the same things two and three times. Damn it, I was going in circles! This was not only a fair analogy for my life, but it was also the last straw for me. I got directions from a local, and by the time I finally found the station, I wholeheartedly agreed with Voice 2—*I had to stop drinking*. I got a ticket to Munich and was off to the train gate number.

Inside the station, I was mesmerized by the trains, how many there were, and how fast they were going! I moved closer to the track to see when the next train was coming. I looked right then left, then suddenly felt another train, a very long one whiz by me really fast. It created a sort of a suction effect and OH SHIT! I was suddenly pulled down toward the tracks. THE FUCK!

I quickly looked to see if another train was coming. A young man reached down to help me up and away from the tracks. He pulled me up, and I dusted myself off.

"My name is Hendrich," he said. "Are you OK?"

I muttered a few swear words and gave him a huge thank-you! It turned out that we were heading in the same direction, and we both caught the next train. During our ride, he invited me to his home for a visit. What! How could I refuse? He had likely saved my life, and I needed all the good luck I could find!

About an hour later, we arrived in a small city where Hendrich lived. It turned out that no one was around by the time we reached his home. Hendrich offered me a few snacks, and you guessed it: a drink. We started drinking some excellent local beer. (I know. I know. I am supposed to be going to Munich. And hadn't I just vowed to *stop* drinking?)

Hendrich asked me if I smoked. I replied, Hell no! But do you know how I can score some heroin?

The only surprise was that Hendrich was *not* surprised. He just smiled quickly and replied, "Yes!" He extended his hand to me and said, "I will need 100 USD."

Without further ado, I forked over the money. Hendrich told me to relax, watch TV, and that if anyone came home, to just introduce myself and say I was waiting for him. Hendrich returned later with enough heroin for both of us. We indulged in the "H" and then went to a local party. Although the club was small, it reminded me of a scaled-down rave. Hendrich and I had a blast and danced most of the night. When it was time to go, we found another source for heroin, bought more, than shot back to Hendrich's house for a little goodnight local TV.

I opened my eyes the next morning on Hendrich's couch and told him that I really needed to get to Munich. He made a couple of calls, and a taxi showed up. I got into the cab, but Hendrich only reached in and shook my hand. That would be the last time I saw Hendrich. (Hendrich, if you ever see this, please reach out to me, buddy, and thank you.)

I finally got to the station and boarded a train bound for Munich. Yes, seriously, this time. As I enjoyed the beautiful landscape flashing by outside, I ordered a glass of any alcohol from the usher.

At last, we arrived in Munich! I hopped into a cab and asked to be taken to the Kempinski Hotel. Once I arrived, I was stunned by the size and beauty of this place. I hurried over to the check-in counter, and the lady behind the desk motioned toward my arm and asked if I was okay. Remember, I'm still in the same clothes. My T-shirt is dirty, smelly, torn, and missing one sleeve; my arm was still scraped up and bruised.

I'm okay, I replied. Can I please check-in? I'm with the Audi group. She said, "Oh, Audi. All right."

Before she could say anything else, I asked her if she knew who Cassandra Crawford from the Audi group was and how I could make contact with her.

All of a sudden, it dawned on her, her face said it all, she knew that I was the lost American who never arrived. After some small talk, she verified my identity with my license and motioned me over toward the ballroom and bar area where Audi was having their **end-of-event** dinner party.

Yep, with my bag still hanging across my body, torn shirt, bruised arm, and bloodshot eyes, I had arrived. Inside the ballroom, I saw Cassandra at the bar.

I walked up behind her and said, "Damn, hey, girl?"

She turned around and gave me a huge hug and was shocked that I had turned up. "Ahhhh, my Frankie," she screamed. I reached into my back pocket and ordered us a round of drinks. After all, we had to celebrate my return, right? After Cassandra asked me what happened, I shared my whole story. It wasn't too long and afterwards we all had to turn in because our plane was leaving for San Francisco in a few hours. She got me to my room and I was out like a light.

BANG, BANG, BANG, BANG.

Was that the hotel door?

It was. The door flung open, and there was Cassandra in hysterics. "Frankie, Frankie! C'mon, honey! Get up, get up, baby!"

Cassandra had to ask the front desk to open my door to get my drunken ass up and to the airport. Yes, I was passed the fuck out! Cassandra got me up and somewhat dressed, considering what few choices she had. (Remember, I had no idea where any of my luggage was.) She grabbed my boarding pass from the front desk and got my ass to the airport. I luckily made it through security, and after that, I've drawn a blank.

The next thing I knew, I came to, looked at the person next to me, and asked where I was. "You're on a plane headed for San Francisco," the kind man said.

I thanked him and minded my own business. I tried to focus outside the window the majority of the flight and ordered a drink just to settle down and relax my mind. No, seriously, I needed to chill out mentally. A couple of hours later, I fell asleep again.

After what seemed like a blink of an eye, the flight attendant had to keep nudging me to wake me up. "We've landed, sir," she said. "We're in San Francisco."

I felt my lip quivering, and tears fell down my face. *I'm home! I'm home!* I looked up and thanked God for bringing me back alive. Once outside the airport, I flagged down a blue shuttle van and paid the $75 for the trip to San Jose. The driver asked if I had any luggage. All I could tell him was that I didn't even know what country my luggage was in!

When I got home, I climbed into a hot shower and stood there for about thirty minutes; this was my first shower in over four days! I was so happy to be home, and I couldn't wait to share my experience with some close friends. A good friend of mine at the time introduced me to a friend of his named Nicole. She had been the one I starting talking to before I left on my trip. So naturally, she hadn't heard from me either and through hear-say had thought I was lost as well. I went over to her house and a short while later, our friends Eric and Kelly had stopped by. I shared with them all what I had been through and that my trip was nothing short of a life experience as well as an adventure. The looks on their faces were that of wow and worry. They were all beside themselves and appeared to be grateful that I had returned.

When I finally returned to my job, I told everyone my harrowing story (minus the alcohol and heroin, of course), and I continued to work as usual. After all, my co-workers didn't need to know that I was an addict and an alcoholic. I only wanted them to see me as an asset and nothing else. I managed to convince myself that no one knew the truth. Yet how could any of them *not* have known what I had become? I remember that it was so hard for me to function at times, and I could barely hold myself together.

After my return, I spent from mid-February until March 28, 2011, trying to locate my luggage. That was six weeks and multiple calls to Delta in Atlanta; call after call, email after email. Only through the diligent effort of Nicole (a different Nicole), the baggage loss and recovery employee for Delta was able to get my luggage back to my home city of San Jose. It turns out my suitcases had logged more flight miles then I had in my whole life. Thanks, Nicole! Delta doesn't deserve you.

During that same time, while I was trying to get my luggage back, I pulled another disappearing act. With that, I received word through a couple of personal contacts that I no longer had a job waiting for me, and that my final check was in the mail. Another loss! I knew it, I knew it, I knew it. I had left my Boss no choice but to do what he did, because I abandoned my job and him with it. By the end of my disappearance, I was also trying to kick the habit—quit drinking and doing drugs altogether.

On the morning of March 28th, I went to pick up my luggage at the San Jose Airport. Afterward, I thought it was time to stop by my place of work and man-up to my boss. He deserved at least that much. After shaking a couple of other hands to say goodbye, I knocked on his door and asked if I could have a moment. My body hurt, and I was now on my second day of complete withdrawal. I sat down in front of him, and I realized that I needed to hold back the sorrow and tears that were blooming within. I shared with him who I was and what I had become. I sugar-coated nothing and was upfront with him. I thanked him and sincerely apologized. I then stood up, shook his hand, turned, and started to exit his office when I heard this voice in my head say, "Do I have your attention *now*?"

Quietly, my head nodded up and down in a yes movement.

As you begin to see my turn-around, what will be YOUR turn-around point?

Yes, now I'm listening.

My Why

How many times have we said to ourselves or someone else, "I've had enough!" or "That's it! I'm done! I'm over it, and I'm not taking this shit anymore."

We've probably all used these words at one time or another. You can tell from my story that I said it often. Yet, obviously, I never really meant it, whether I cared to admit it or not. Saying those words isn't the same as committing to them.

I wanted to blame "Life" for my problems. And I would often ask, "Why me? Why is this happening to me?" In hindsight, the answer is pretty simple. I look at it in two ways now: First, because I deserved it. I received what I sent out. Second, what happened to me wasn't really enough. I thought I was mentally tough enough to outlast and prevail through those dark times and appear as the winner on the other side. Yep, a trophy held high.

I could not have been more wrong.

Do you hear what I am saying to you? Do I have your attention? Look, in life, if you are even given another chance, do you just jump on it, or do you ever ask, "Do I deserve it?" Everything that happened to me was **because** of me. I take full responsibility, and

I can write this to you today because I made that U-turn, and you surely can, too.

For those seeking change through recovery, please understand it will not be an easy road. Mental note: It's not supposed to be. Today may not be a good day, but if you quit, if you really stick with it, well, then when the sun sets, you will be one day closer to a happier one, and that will make quitting all the more worth it.

It's going to be the challenge of a lifetime, and to weather this storm, you need a strong, sturdy anchor to motivate and inspire you. So, ask yourself: what do you want more than anything? What is it, for as sure as you can breathe, that you want most in life? What is your drive, who or what are you willing to do ANYTHING for? Do you have a purpose, something greater than yourself that yearns for your complete and undivided attention? You'll need that. It's your **WHY,** and I found mine.

Years ago, on that sunny Friday morning in March, just after I picked up my long-lost luggage and said goodbye to my boss, I made a decision. If you recall, I made amends with my boss. I had gone in, shook my boss's hand, and began to exit when I heard that voice say, "Do I have your attention now?" Well, before I got to my car, I was already in full tears. I recognized that I was at the bottom. Right at that moment, I had what I had always considered a great reason to pop pills or splash some whiskey on my teeth to escape my feelings.

Instead, I whispered back, "Yes, you have my attention now, and I will be a student of change."

That weekend I had a very tough time; I have never ever wanted to drink or crush pills more than that weekend. I struggled. I struggled hard. But my **WHY** kept me in line, and would not allow me to deter from my goal: *quitting*. Nicole, the woman I saw at the time, actually had no idea what was really going on, so that meant

I had to go it alone. My inner circle did what they could for me, and of course, I had given them many reasons to stay back, but in this end, they would be there for me emotionally and physically, yet from a distance, at least for now. And what more could I ask?

I remember one night during this time as I was driving; Christina called me to see how I was doing. At this time, I was trying to process how I was going to go about this whole sobriety thing and how it was going to affect others around me. I completely opened up to her. I know she had heard these same things from me thousands of times before, but somehow, she sensed this conversation was different, was more genuine. Christina said, "I heard Nicole drinks, and that's not good for you, Franklin." I said, yes, she does, but I wouldn't ask her to stop because of me, and I firmly believe anything she does would not be a temptation for me. I said she drinks nothing like me and has on an occasional drink here and there. You know, wine and beer, but nothing like me. She then said with a subtle pause, "Alright, Franklin." Christina and I spoke a little more and ended the conversation by agreeing that I needed to *show her* that I could change. Chris deserved change, and most of all so did our girls.

If I can come through the hell of my life, I firmly believe you can too. It starts by identifying your **WHY** and pursuing the many different avenues of help that are available to you. I've read the *Big Book of Alcoholics Anonymous by Dr. Bob Smith and Bill Wilson* (affectionately known as the "*Big Blue Book*"), and I've attended group and recovery home fellowships. I am actually a friend of *Bill's*, although we don't see things in quite the same way. I took fragments of the Big Blue Book and opted to do things MY way, although I don't advise this for everyone. *The Bible*—specifically the entire book of *Proverbs*—really helped me get on my track; it applies to both the spiritual and non-spiritual side of life. *Spoiler alert!* If you do read the book of *Proverbs*, you may become spiritual afterward.

Since I'm making a strong point about having a **WHY**, it's only fair that I share mine with you—if you haven't already guessed. My **WHY** is my daughters Lauryn and Ysabella. As a baby, I don't really remember the feeling of having a father abandon me—ultimately, I vowed that I was *not* going to leave them with that same feeling. That was *not* going to be the legacy I bequeathed to them.

I called Lauryn and apologized for what I had become. I don't think I ever really told her or described myself to her as a "drunken addict". At the time, she was still young, so I just used the phrase "dad and his wrongdoings" to describe my sad actions. Lauryn was smart, very smart. Bless her heart, that beautiful little girl was a trooper. She never once looked at me with ill will, even during visiting hours at the psych ward. I am indebted to her feelings of empowerment towards me and for allowing me to become the best father for her and her little sister.

That same end of March weekend, I promised her during a phone call that the way she currently knew me would not be the man I would become.

I said while I was crying, Lauryn, baby, daddy loves you and sister so much, and I haven't been the father you both deserve. I am so sorry and from now on, if you can forgive me, I promise to be the best dad that you both deserve, and one day you will be proud of me and not embarrassed to say that's my dad. I love you, Lauryn.

She said, "Thank you. I love you, Daddy."

I fell out. I couldn't keep the tears back. I cried hard, and then my voice cracked even more as I continued to tell Lauryn how much I loved her and how much she meant to me.

She knew I'd broken down, and she said, "It will be okay, Daddy."

I had to quickly end the call because I couldn't hold the torrent of emotions inside. That's the power of your **Why**. It becomes the strength you can call on to break through anything and everything that might stand in the way of your recovery. My **Why** was more significant than me; the love and respect of my girls was the drive I needed to pierce through the noise of a demon's chant. My **Why** allowed me to feel the affection of my girls, that same affection would become the lifesaving touch that massaged my *refurbished soul.*

Ascension

L et what I have shared be proof that no matter what you have gone through, there will always be a small flickering within you that can be fanned into the flames of change. I genuinely believe you weren't born just to exist; you weren't born to be average… you were born to be brilliant and do amazing things. If you want to change and you genuinely believe that you can change, well, then you will.

Tao Te Ching once said *when the student is ready, the master will appear*. And what most do not know is the second half of that quote, and it is; *When the student is ready, the master will disappear.*

I believe to be a student in recovery is to gain enlightenment through self-discipline and mastery. I mean to really master your self- awareness.

And to develop keen situational-awareness skills, which all develop from within. Ask yourself; what commitments can you positively impose upon yourself today? How can you begin to create a discipline for yourself to invite greatness into your life? What foundations within can you start to rebuild during your ascension?

First and foremost: STOP! Stop doing whatever is bad for you, your body, or your spirit. You know exactly what I mean. Don't pretend or lie to yourself, or make excuses and say, "Well, Frank didn't mention *this*, or he didn't mention *that*, so I can still sneak that in."

You CAN'T!

You need to stop disrupting your greatness! Get into alignment.

Listen to me; stand up, shoulders back, and keep your chin up as you head forward into your better future. Make a commitment to stop, then begin to discipline and learn about your new self. Yes, you can start with baby steps. Teach yourself new and subtle ways of doing things while you adhere to the basics of the discipline. Part of my commitment was that I told those close to me that one day I would be twice the man they remembered before I was lost. Twice, the man! That meant I needed to begin with self-discipline and start from scratch.

Through my own cognitive dissonance, I needed to undo and redo what I had learned growing up in the military, and as a young adult so I can coach myself back to greatness. For example, the approach I took was of the most basic, disciplined, and un- recovery-like way through getting clean: mind, body, and *refurbished soul.*

So, what I am about to share is how I did it, and you are more than welcome to use, borrow, or emulate in any which way you choose. Or simply design your path to change.

Here is how I did it, prefaced by; La méthode Coué (The Coué method). The Coué method is a litany of this magical expression, **"Every day, in every way, I'm getting better and better,"** twenty times in the morning, and twenty times at the end of each day. I chose to say it all throughout the days.

Then-

» I taught myself to tie my shoes right over left because I grew up left over right. (A baby step in relearning a habit.)

» I stopped swearing and disallowed any hostile words coming from my mouth. (Allowing love to move closer to me.)

» I re-taught myself to quit eating meat, which I loved. (minimizing GMO into my body and allowing my digestive system a bit of ease. After all, it had been through enough.)

» I went to the gym 5 days a week, including detoxing in the steam room. (this one is mandatory to relieve your body of all the toxins within you.)

» I consciously tried to reconnect with the love inside me and kept away evil thoughts. (I needed to replace the evil within, with love I yearned for.)

» I lent myself out to others. I assisted in outside counseling for other people; twice, I wrote wedding vows for people. I made a few hospital visits to those who needed me to oversee their loved ones at the beginning of their own recovery. Sometimes what qualified me to help others was that I could also teach them what NOT to do. I was also blessed with the opportunity to lead a few of my friends to start their own businesses or be better at their current ones. Two are still going strong; the others quit on themselves. (Allowing all to heal.)

» I stopped drinking coffee, and any other beverages that I felt had a pull on me. (I allow myself to drink coffee today, but it is no longer the master of my morning. Proving to myself who is always in charge.)

» During my first six months of getting clean, I woke up at 0350 a few times a week, so that I could swim quietly in the pool of my apartment complex. Yes, it was cold, but I was stretching and rebuilding the outside of my comfort zone. (this shook my body, and allowed me to prove I was in charge of the moment.)

» I would take walks down the same streets that I had walked when I was drunk or high. While walking, I said small prayers to myself, acknowledging to the demons that they had lost their hold on me because now I had hold of myself. This internally allowed me to carve a different path than the one I was demonically known for. (Making amends with the spirits that dwelled on the sidewalks I walked on.)

» Finally, I read inspiring books that would help reteach my inner being how to once again put myself first and show me how to massage my *Refurbished Soul* back to a loving state. (Basic teaching to rejuvenate my inner self.)

Have a look at just a FEW of the books that helped me:

» *Your Best Life Now* by Joel Osteen

» *The Four Agreements* by Don Miguel Ruiz

» *Outwitting The Devil* by Napoleon Hill

» *AA Big Book* by Bill W.

» *Lessons from San Quentin* by Bill Dallas

» *A Purpose Driven Life* by Rick Warren

» Three books by John Maxwell
   ○ *Make Today Count*
   ○ *The 5 Levels of Leadership*
   ○ *How Successful People Think*

» *90 Minutes in Heaven* by Don Piper/Cecil Murphy

» *The Strangest Secret* by Earl Nightingale

» Two books by Marianne Williamson
  ○ *A Return to Love*
  ○ *The Law of Divine Compensation.*

Along with two books by two women that I just adore and who helped lead me in the direction of writing and finishing this book:

» *Big Magic: Creative Living Beyond Fear* by Elizabeth Gilbert

» *The Power of Vulnerability* by Brene Brown.

Yes, of course, there are others, and I'm sure you'll find even more that speak to you in your ascension back to your inner light. Audiobooks can also be of great help, but whichever version you use, don't read or play it just once. Keep learning each time you read or listen again. Over, and over, and over.

What's my message? I did whatever it took to RESET my internal disciplinary culture. I ventured out of my comfort zone to teach myself, my body, and my brain to stretch and relearn things that I did each day. Yes, that included changing even the smallest of habits. I was literally reconstructing my habitual disciplines.

My only way out of the hell which I created was to take full responsibility for me, and ultimately re-teach myself. The military taught me that every day was a Monday. I changed that paradigm and taught myself instead, that every day is a Friday. Celebrate and *Grind!*

Wayne Dyer once said, "*Change the way you look at things and the things you look at change.*" This too, was a staple in my world. I mentioned before, it was during one of my psychology classes years earlier that I also memorized a saying by French psychologist Émile Coué that has since helped me tremendously: "*Every day in every way, I am getting better and better.*" I even got a tattoo of this quote on my arm to always remind myself.

Coué practiced around the turn of the century (1900) and introduced autosuggestion as a means of self-improvement. He would prescribe a placebo that tricked patients into thinking that the "medication" was making them better when it was only the power of their mind that healed them. I am a big advocate of autosuggestion; it's been one of the main deciding factors in my own ascension into Self-Mastery.

I also firmly believe that it was only when I had nothing, did I truly want to attract something good and positive. Some people call that "rock bottom." And some ask what now?

Key moment.

It was at this time, and during a part of a rocky recovery, that the Lord threw me a life preserver.

I was broken in about as many different ways as you can be, plus jobless and sitting in a business class at San Jose City College. I was so immersed in what the teacher was sharing that it took a classmate to notify me that my phone was vibrating. I received a text from December during class and chanced opening it. The text read something like, "Kevin wants you back at BMW." That exploded my mind; I was momentarily locked onto the phone screen. I kept still, and that alarmed my classmate, so she asked, everything ok? To which I said, uh, yeah, thanks. I was so excited that I could no longer focus on my class. This was a tremendous blessing and opportunity; a chance to press CTRL-ALT-DELETE on my past and forge a new future. This literally could not have come at a better time.

Was this redemption? For me, it felt like redemption with four shots of vindication, venti-sized! Kevin was the GM at the BMW dealership and one of my best friends. He knew me, he really knew what I was about inside and out, and he had witnessed my past. I will never forget that night when he extended his hand to me via December's text. In a lifetime where I had been offered many

Take note: going to "therapy" is not an automatic "Get Out of Jail Free" card. You need to find the right therapist; you may talk to a whole list of people just to find one who fits you. Consider it recruitment to find *the right player for your team.* I spent countless hours with the wrong therapists. Even now, I'm still looking. Group and Twelve Steps didn't work for me because I wouldn't allow them to work. I wanted a harder way: one that took more discipline and white knuckles. But in addition to my search, I also seek counsel through self-determination and a simple rule: if it looks, smells or even sounds wrong—*then it is and not for me, I stay in alignment...*

I still often walk through the liquor aisle at the grocery stores, running the backside of my hands across the shelves of bottles, while listening to my nails go *ting, ting, ting* all the way down the aisle. Is that flirting with temptation? I think so, but I've disciplined myself to stay in complete control and reignite that core of who I have become. I'm often asked, "Frank, don't you wish you could drink and not turn into an alcoholic again?"

The truth of the matter is: YES. Yes, I do. However, life doesn't work that way, and that path is not part of my repayment plan for a durable finish in life. My daughters deserve my utmost best at all times, and I made a promise to Lauryn that I would never go south again!

I will keep that promise and ensure that my grandkids will always have something good to say about me... *and mean it.*

I give one hundred and ten percent of myself every day to make sure I don't backtrack down the depths of my own hell. I keep my mind and *refurbished soul* locked in a vault and surrendered the key to God, who has delivered me from evil, just like the hymns promised in church with Bishop Anderson. No more drinking "because I earned it." My five days a week at the gym are my reward now, and each day reminds me that I am once again allowed to love and live again.

Unbreakable! That's my mentality now. Hard work and "yes, sir!" are my replenished habits. I give my best at everything because that was part of my promise years ago. It was my deal with God, along with my commitment to Lauryn and her little sister.

When I look back at the jobs I lost and the roles that redeemed me, my employers were both gambling and smart. These key players remembered the Frank they knew before I fell, and they gambled big time again. It paid off for all of us; they both won! One had the vision of me becoming great, led my charge, and the other brought it to fruition. I recently graduated from the National Automobile Dealers Associations General Managers' academy. I gave these men each a return on their investment. I repaid them both in full and nothing on credit!

Love, Belief and Me

In the end, this is my story. I wrote these pages of a cautionary tale to share my hard-learned lessons with anyone who cares to listen: it's never too late to do a 180 in life.

I have rewritten the secret code to which I now function on. I had to, I needed to include it within the new internal software that I am love and with this love comes belief. I have known, and even more, now that I am but a small minuscule atom in this universe, and with this firm belief, faith then exists.

You see most of us grew up thinking that our beliefs are what our parents and people told us; how we grew up and how the world saw us would later form the beliefs into who we think we are today. Well, I was convinced, and we all agreed that I had become a drunken addict to which, yes, I made this vision of many who saw me come true, and ultimately my own reality.

We have all heard people say, "It's not the destination that counts, but it's the journey." Well, in *my* world, you can't have one without the other anyway. I see it as— to get any kind of real reward in life, you must first pay the price. You will only receive in direct proportion to what you've paid or given.

It occurs to me that I'm not in recovery from drugs or alcohol as much as I am in the restoration of love and self-respect. I didn't love or respect myself enough to morally correct the bad decisions that led me down the wrong roads. I didn't love myself enough to feel; I didn't realize I had personal worth. No self-respect. Nothing of value for Christina, or the girls.

Yes, I still think about substances today. But I think of love and self-discipline more! I think about both so much that I require almost an hourly accountability each day, a running ledger of who am I, and what am I doing. I remind myself throughout each day that I have more love for myself today than I did yesterday. For, without this, I'm unable to be the best for myself, family, and friends.

Every day I need to reach down deep enough to say, Frank. I love you. Frank, I forgive you. Frank, I need you to keep pushing forward at all costs.

Voice 2 whispers happily in my head with nothing but encouragement; "Resurrect your name; enable your daughters to smile when they hear it spoken; leave a mark within people that will fill their hearts long after you have passed. Leave all of whom you come into contact with, better than before you met them."

I listen more closely now—to both verbal and non-verbal communications. I see differently; I've been blessed through enlightenment.

If you don't listen, you will! And if you don't listen now, you'll keep speeding down the wrong road as I did… you have seen what it cost me and what will it cost YOU?

No matter what you have been through, you can change where you're going and how you'll get there. Don't try to calm yourself; *be afraid!* Be afraid enough to know that your next lousy decisions could result in death—not always physically, but mentally and soulfully, or they could cause the end of valuable relationships that you hold dearest.

It is now time for me to give back to all who emotionally and physically invested in me, to everyone who stuck with me, and called to see how I was doing. I love and appreciate everyone inside my inner circle. I am grateful that you took my drunk and wasted calls and saw past what I was mumbling. You allowed me to prove my real self to you, my true feelings to you, and you made me do it all through actions. To all who believed in me...

Welcome to the return on your investment!

I love you.

Thank you for allowing me to share.

ACKNOWLEDGMENTS

My Daughters Lauryn and Ysabella

WOW! My beautiful and amazing young daughters, I am so proud to say I am your Daddy. I am truly grateful for your continued love and for allowing me to remain in your lives. I honestly would not have made it out without your soft touches and warm embraces. Because of you, I have received another chance to make my life count. YOU ARE MY **WHY**! I love you both so much!

Christina

Chris, thank you for your sternness throughout all of this. I am genuinely grateful that you knew just how much rope to allow me. I appreciate who and what you are to the girls and me; you helped keep my emotions in a stable place, and I am forever indebted.

Richie

I love you, man, thank you for sticking by my side and allowing me my space to find out for myself. I appreciate all you have done for me, both emotionally and physically, through our friendship.

Kevin

What can I say, Kev? We did it, and I am so thankful for you, allowing me to be your friend, and for allowing me to break out of that worn-out skin to become the man, you knew I could be. Thank you for the second chance.

December

I thank you for putting up with me when I couldn't even put up with myself. Thank you for sticking in there, when, at times, I didn't want to clean up or live. Thank you for the subtle whispers of "Everything's going to be okay." Thank you for putting our friendship first, exactly how we agreed long ago.

Cassandra

I appreciate your unconditional love and for allowing me to come back into your world. I would probably still be in Germany if you didn't wake my ass up and get me on that plane. Thanks girl, mad love!

Danielle

Thank you for your love and for coming to my rescue whenever I called.

Nicole

Thank you for allowing me the space to conquer my demons; I realize I'm not your typical guy, but then again, who wants one of those?

Dr. Jerry Callaway

Sir, I appreciate you so much, and I am grateful that you were there for me when most other doctors seemed to want to push more drugs on me. Thank you for opening up your office to me and keeping your gatekeeper away. I owe you, sir.

Joseph

Thank you for insisting that you gain entrance into my apartment that day. I don't know where I would be now if you and Richie didn't persist. Thanks, Joey!

Tony

What up, Boss? Thank you for trying to rescue me in the beginning. I am so grateful for your confidence in me to make a comeback, apply for life's redemption, and be stamped for approval.

Curtis

Thank you for the prayers and the nonjudgmental friendship that you provided along with your open heart. Thank you for that talk on the way to the Veterans' Hospital.

Rachel

I am grateful that you accepted me unconditionally, and you were there for me when I needed you.

My Family Circle: my mother, my Lil brother Eric, Aunt Chris, my cousin Janeen, my in-laws Ray & Carol, Raymond, Briana, Gregory, Rita, Lyndsey, Ruben, Mike, Lisa and Lisa, Alyssa, Josh, Anton, Uncle Joey, Stacy, Pippa, Uncle Cliff, Aunty June.

I greatly appreciate all of you who have allowed me to remain a part of your family. I will forever be indebted to you. Thank you for all of the Christmases. I would not have made it this far without each of you doing your part!

My BMW circle: Nancy, Lil Jen, Connie, Sherry, Joe, Gil, Steve H., and Romeo

I am so grateful to have all of you in my world; you all proved to me that you loved me then, and you love me now.

My MBZ circle: Barry F. (aka B-Fro), Des, The Dotsons-Adeajai and Lukman, Sammie, and Mark

Thank you for accepting me when I was going down. I appreciate you all, and thank you for staying in touch with me and showing that you genuinely care.

My Audi circle: James, Cindy, Cass, Ernie, and Jairo

I appreciate you all welcoming me back and allowing me to become what I am today.

Stephanie Wong

Thank you for not judging me after seeing the other side. I am so grateful for your guidance in editing parts of my book during its infancy. You were the first to view it. You mean a lot to me, and thank you for you.

Kelly and E

Thank you for being there for me early on in my transition to sobriety and for not judging me, along with allowing me to be of service to both of you.

Laura and Abby

(the two anesthesiologists) on our plane ride home from Detroit

Thanks for reading and providing your opinion. It was warming to see both of your faces when were done reading my initial chopped up version of this book. I thank both of you.

My editors: R. Lee Brown, Mary Thomas and Judi Blaze

Thank you all so much for your insight and belief in me to get my message out and for providing me the guidance to becoming an Author.

Dr. Chapa

Thank you for the literary discipline that you showed me and for allowing me to make mistakes while recognizing that I was working on my craft. You allowed me the mental space to break through and understand what was within me. You taught me the value of getting my teeth kicked in as you broke down and replaced lifelong habits. I appreciate you Sir.

Made in the USA
Middletown, DE
14 November 2021